Bible Games for Children

BY

JENNY BROWN

EASTBOURNE

Other titles in this series:

To Katie
who, as well as being a fantastic friend,
unknowingly helped to inspire the compilation
of this book as she worked week after week
with some lively Edinburgh children.

ISBN 1 - 84291 - 129 - 5
Published by Kingsway Communications Ltd,
26 Lottbridge Drove, Eastbourne, East Sussex BN23 6NT

Cover design and production for the publishers by
Bookprint Creative Services
P.O. Box 827, BN21 3YJ, England.
Printed in Great Britain.

Contents

Safety Notice

All of the games and activities in this book have, in principle, been tried and tested (some over many years), but we urge all readers to exercise great care when encouraging children to run or handle objects which could cause harm to them if swallowed, misused, etc.

Acknowledgements

A big thank you once again to the team at Children's Ministry — this has been a joint project which would not have been completed without you. Special thanks to Cathy Kyte and Sue Price for their helpful input throughout the whole book; to Ruth Alliston particularly for her contributions to the ideas for younger children; and to Andy Back for being fun to work with. Thanks to Andy for compiling the Bible index and theme index and for editing and correcting the manuscript.

Thanks also to the sales team at our Eastbourne office (at the time of writing: Phil, Mary, Gemma and Neil) — you all have such an enthusiastic, helpful attitude and a fantastic ability to communicate which resources will suit which leaders, children, churches and age groups. Thanks for helping us write materials which are wanted and for feeding back useful information from the hundreds of people to whom you speak.

Finally, thank you to all the leaders and children who, before we'd ever thought of writing this book, contributed by playing many of the games which form the basis of these 100 ideas.

Introduction

Do you, like many children's leaders as they prepare for their forthcoming children's ministry session, wrack your brains for a game you can play with your children? You know that children love to play and that enjoyment is key to their time with you. If they don't enjoy themselves they will either refuse to come or cause trouble. Sometimes you'll play a game at the start or finish of a session, 'just for fun'. However, a game that links with your story and theme is invaluable. In fact, a game can be the best way for children to take in and process the key point of your session.

Many children, including all young children and a large proportion of boys of all ages, need to move in order to learn. They are the so-called bodily-kinesthetic or tactile-kinesthetic learners. At Children's Ministry all our resources take into account the differing learning styles of children, but we place a particular emphasis on children 'doing', not just watching and listening. The connections in children's brains that store and process information will develop most efficiently if they physically act out what they are learning through drama, dance, games or art and craft activities. Actually, scientific fact backs up what we can see from the Bible – when God has something important for his people (of any age) to remember, he often gives us something to do, for example, the festivals of the Old Testament, or the sharing of bread and wine.

For the most active and competitive children, games and sport will be their favourite way of learning. But all children like to play and so the game element will probably be the most popular part of your Bible teaching session for the majority of the children. For a more detailed explanation of the benefits of using action, games, sports and movement and for advice and ideas regarding specific age groups see the companion to this book, the *Children's Ministry Guide to Fun and Games for Active Learning* (Children's Ministry, 2003).

The following pages contain games for 100 of some of the most popular Old and New Testament Bible stories. Most are very active games. The children will love it if you join in but don't worry if you can't - you can still organise them perfectly well from the sidelines. Some are taken from, or adapted from, the *Children's Ministry Teaching Programme*; others are new. Of course, some of the games are well known, or at least adapted from a well-known game. However, the purpose of this book is not just to provide you with a list of games but to show how the games can link with Bible stories so that the children will learn important biblical truth as they play.

The definitions of a 'game', according to the Collins English Dictionary, include 'an amusement or pastime; diversion;' and 'a contest with rules, the result being determined by skill, strength or chance.' While many of the games in this book do take the form of a contest with rules and result in a winner or winning team, other activities come under the broader definition of a game where the aim is fun and not necessarily competition.

For each Bible story game in this book, you will find:

A biblical reference
Games in the first half of the book (linked to Old Testament stories) are in biblical order. Games in the second half of the book are grouped according to aspects of the life of Jesus and the early church, starting with Jesus' birth, moving through his life and teaching, continuing to his death and resurrection and finishing with the birth of the church. The whole passage relating to the story is given, but often you will use a shortened version of the story in the session, as in the *Children's Ministry Teaching Programme*.

There is little reference to the 'non-story' parts of the Bible such as Psalms, Proverbs and the letters of the New Testament as this book specifically focuses on games linked with stories, generally the most suitable parts to use with under 11s. See *100 Fun Ways to teach the Bible to children* by Cathy Kyte (Children's Ministry, 2003) for more ideas using verses from these books.

A key verse
The key verse can be used as a memory verse. Sometimes you may wish to use a shortened version, and sometimes you will want to replace it with a verse of your own choosing.

A list of connected themes
A theme index at the back of the book will help you to find a passage and a game for a wide variety of biblical themes. If you can't find a game for the passage you are using, look in the theme index as there may be something suitable or adaptable linked with another story.

A clearly stated aim for the game
Some games act as an introduction to the Bible story, in which case you'll play the game first. Others are to reinforce

the story, or help the children remember the key points, and these are best used as follow-up activities. Others emphasise or help the children understand a theme or key point, and can be used before or after the story.

Notes for preparation of the game
Here you will find any equipment necessary and any other preparations needed.

Instructions regarding how to play the game
This section tells you how to organise the children. Most games will work best with a practice run-through first. Remember children are often happy to play a game again and again. Don't worry about using the same game again on another occasion.

Sometimes a specific prize is suggested which links with the game or theme. Don't feel you have to give prizes out after every game and be careful about allergies if you give sweets or anything else edible.

Children are very happy to receive 'points' that can be totalled at the end of the session, month, half term, etc. and then exchanged for a prize. Children over the age of about six generally like to compete.

Try to ensure the winners change frequently. Three or more teams are generally better than two if possible, so that you don't just have 'winners' and 'losers'. First, second and third sounds better! Encourage the children to support each other and not to boast about their own achievements or ridicule others.

An application paragraph
This helps you to teach a key fact, helps you to explain to the children how the game links with the Bible passage, and

often relates the game and story to the children's lives. This is provided as what you might say to the children, and so to maintain our usual style, this is given in bold type.

For younger children
Most of the games will be most suitable for 7-11's (some will stretch to teens or adults) but the paragraph at the bottom of each game idea will give you ideas about how to adapt the game for younger children. It may give a very different idea if the main game will not adapt easily. Many team games and some with more complicated instructions will be difficult with under-7s. If for some reason you don't think your group will enjoy the main game idea, check out the 'For Younger Children' section in case you prefer that idea. The application paragraph will normally need changing somewhat if you use the option for younger children.

Note for front-led groups: if you are working with a very large number of children, where you largely rely on front-led activities, it may not be possible for every individual to participate in each game. In this case, choose a smaller group to take part at the front and involve the others as much as possible in cheering them on, chanting, clapping, etc.

I hope you enjoy playing these games with your children. Change and adapt them to make them more suitable for your group and look out for board games, games on the TV and anything fun and energetic that you could make into your own new game. God has designed children to learn through play so always remember that all your games are more than 'just for fun'!

1

Seven Days

Genesis 1:1-31; 2:1-3

Key verse: God saw all that he had made and it was very good (Genesis 1:31).

Theme: Creation.

Aim: To help the children remember all God made each day in the story of creation.

Preparation:

For each team you will need a large die plus a set of pictures depicting what God made on each day of Creation. These can be cut from magazines, photocopied or drawn. Mount or draw each set on six sectors of a circle and cut out the sectors.

How to play:

Teams of four to six children sit in a circle and take it in turns to roll a die. As soon as someone rolls a '1', they may run to the middle of the room and find one of the pictures that represent 'light and dark'. They bring this back to the middle of the team. Meanwhile the rest of the team continues to roll the die. When someone rolls a '2', they may run to the middle of the room and find one of the pictures that represent 'sky'. They bring this back to the middle of the team.

The game continues in the same way until the children have collected pictures representing 'sea and land, plants and trees', 'stars, sun and moon', 'birds and fish' and 'animals and people'. They should then be able to make a circle with their sectors.

They should shout 'Creation' when they have finished. Remind the children that you only have pictures for six days because on the seventh day, God rested.

God created everything in an orderly way. He made everything on earth – sea, land, plants and animals, human beings – and everything in the universe – all the stars and planets, the sun and the moon. They don't just exist by accident - God made them.

For younger children:
Remove the competitive element. Give each group their own set of pictures near to their team circle.

2

God's Creative Power

Genesis 1:1-31

Key verse: In the beginning God created the heavens and the earth (Genesis 1:1).

Theme: Creation.

Aim: To emphasize the extent of God's power and creativity in Creation.

Preparation:

You will need a set of ten pieces of card for each pair or small group. Each card must have one of the words or phrases **in bold** written on it.

1 The coldest place in the world is in **Antarctica**.
2 The driest place in the world is in **Chile**.
3 The hottest place in the world is in **Libya**.
4 The wettest place in the world is in **India**.
5 The biggest wave ever seen was caused by an earthquake in Alaska. Its height was approximately **500 metres**.
6 The depth of the deepest parts of the sea is about **7 miles**.
7 The biggest river, in terms of how much water it carries, is the Amazon. It's length is about **4000 miles**.
8 The number of stars in creation must be at least equal to **the number of grains of sand on all the beaches of the world.**
9 The biggest star measured, which is 700 times bigger than the Sun, has a diameter of **610 million miles**.
10 Our galaxy, one of billions, spins at 490 000 miles per hour. To make one rotation takes **200 million years**.

How to play:
Form pairs or small groups at one end of the room. Place each group's set of cards at the other end of the room. A leader reads out each of the sentences above, leaving out the word or phrase in bold. One person from each pair or small group then runs to their set of cards. He chooses which card matches that sentence, brings it back to his group and writes the sentence number on it. Have a leader available to help with reading if necessary. Give a small prize to any group that has all the answers correct.

A similar game can be played relating to God's creativity. Below are some facts you could use:

1 The biggest spider, toe to toe, can measure up to **28cm**.
2 The biggest butterfly, wingtip to wingtip, can measure up to **28cm**.
3 The bird that weighs only 1.4 g and can fly backwards and upside down is the **bee hummingbird**.
4 The giant anaconda snake can grow as long as **six children lying end to end**.
5 The reptile that can turn many different colours is the **chameleon**.
6 The pitcher plant is unusual because it eats **insects**.
7 The giant rafflesia flower is unusual because it can be **over 1.5m wide**.
8 The deep-sea anglerfish swims at depths of **over 2,700 metres**.
9 The spiny anteater is an unusual mammal because it **lays eggs**.
10 The bird that builds a nest that looks like a hanging basket is the **weaver bird**.

God created the world and the whole universe. Isn't he amazing? He made the biggest things and the smallest

things. He made so many types of plants and animals. He made the world with hot, cold, wet and dry places. He is so powerful – we can see his power in the strongest winds and the biggest waves.

For younger children:
Use easier facts for younger children. Organise a picture matching activity along similar lines.

3

Mirror Images

Genesis 1:26-27

Key verse: So God created man in his own image, in the
               image of God he created him; male and female
               he created them (Genesis 1:27).

Theme: Creation.

Aim: To introduce the concept of an 'image', prior to
               teaching that we are made in the image of God.

How to play:

Ask group members to form pairs and to stand facing each
other. Ask each pair to choose an activity to mime, such as
washing their face and brushing their teeth. One in each pair
must pretend to be the mirror image of the other. They can
then swap over.

   Which pair can perform the fastest or most complicated
movements whilst still being good mirror images? Award a
prize to the best pair.

**When we look in the mirror we see our reflection, or our
'image'. Our image is just like us. God made Adam and
Eve in his image. That means they were like him. But it
wasn't that they looked exactly like him. It was more
that they were like him in the sort of person they were
and different from all the other creatures God made.**

For younger children:

Provide a mirror. Keep movements simple.

4

Deception

Genesis 3:1-24

Key verse: He [the serpent] said to the woman, 'Did God really say, 'You must not eat from any tree in the garden'?' (Genesis 3:1)

Theme: Sin.

Aim: To emphasize that God tells us what is best for us whereas Satan tries to trick and deceive us.

Preparation:

Set up a simple obstacle course using tables, chairs, etc. You will also need a blindfold, a plastic beaker of water and a plastic bottle/jug.

How to play:

Select a volunteer who will negotiate the course blindfolded while carrying a cup of water. The water must be poured into a bottle at the other end. Select two 'callers' who will be responsible for guiding the volunteer through the course.

Tell the volunteer that one caller will give good instructions, the other bad. As the volunteer finds his/her way through the course, one caller will try to help him/her avoid the obstacles and walk to the other end without spilling the water. They will give clear, simple instructions. The other caller will try to make the volunteer go in the wrong direction, bump into obstacles and spill the water. This caller's instructions can include phrases such as 'Don't listen to him!' and 'Watch out! You'll crash into a table!'

Select other groups of three and measure to see which volunteer collects the most water in the bottle at the end of the course.

God gave Adam and Eve good instructions but the snake gave them bad instructions. God tells us what is best for us whereas Satan tries to trick and deceive us.

For younger children:
Omit the obstacles and use a jug or bucket at the end instead of a bottle. Any children who are nervous about wearing a blindfold may feel happier if they can hold a leader's hand as they walk.

5

Crouching Sin

Genesis 4:1-16

Key verse: But if you do not do what is right, sin is crouch-
                ing at your door; it desires to have you, but you
                must master it (Genesis 4:7).

Themes: Temptation; sin.

Aim: To help the children remember God's words to
                Cain (verse 7) and of how easy it is to get caught
                up in sin.

Preparation:

Ensure you have a clear playing space.

How to play:

This activity will work most easily with six players, but could
be adapted for more or less.

One player stands in the middle of the room. Four players, numbered one to four, crouch, sprint-start style, one
beside each wall, facing the player in the centre.

A sixth person is positioned in one corner with a die.
They roll the die and shout out the number showing.

When players one to four hear their number, they run
towards the centre player and try to tag him.

The centre player, when they hear a number, must run to
any of the four walls and touch it before they are tagged.

It will be best if they run to the opposite wall to that
called.

If a numbered player tags the centre player, they swap

places. If not, the centre player remains in the middle.

When a five or a six is called, either have no one run, or have numbers four and one run when a five is called, and numbers four and two run when a six is called.

It's very easy to do things wrong. It's as though sin is like a cat waiting to pounce on us. If we move in the wrong direction and start doing things wrong, sin will grab hold of us and it can be hard to get out of its grip. Once Cain started to do things wrong, sin got hold of him and things got worse and worse.

For younger children:
Play with three players and just two walls to run to. A leader can simply call 'one' or 'two'.

6

Spot the Difference

Genesis 6:5-22

Key verse: Noah was a righteous man, blameless among the
people of his time, and he walked with God
(Genesis 6:9).

Themes: Obedience; holiness.

Aim: To introduce the topic of difference. Noah was
different from the people around him.

How to play:

Sit the group in a circle and ask everyone to look carefully at
everyone else. After a few moments chose a volunteer to go
out of the room. While they are out, choose one or two
people to change the way they look. For example, changing
hair style or physical position or removing their glasses.

The volunteer then returns and tries to spot the difference. If they do, choose another volunteer. If they don't,
reveal the difference and let them have another go.

**Noah was different from the people around him. It was
not to do with how he looked but how he behaved. The
other people living at that time were evil but Noah lived
a life that pleased God.**

For younger children:

Make the changes more obvious – two people could swap
jumpers, or even swap places.

7

Rainbow Colours

Genesis 9:1-17

Key verse: I have set my rainbow in the clouds, and it will
be the sign of the covenant between me and the
earth (Genesis 9:13).

Theme: Promises.

Aim: To help the children remember God's promise
to Noah.

Preparation:

You will need seven balls of wool in rainbow colours. Cut
sufficient sets of seven lengths for your expected number of
groups.

How to play:

Form pairs or small groups in different corners of the room.
In the middle of the room is a pile of wool, cut into lengths
of different rainbow colours.

Group members take it in turns to run to the middle and
collect a strand of wool, a different colour each time. They
should end up with seven different colours.

To finish the game, these must be tied together (not
twisted) to make one long strand, with the colours in the
order they would be found in a rainbow.

They could even make the lengths, when tied together,
equal the width of the ark (75 feet, so each length of wool
needs to be about 11 feet long).

Groups shout 'rainbow!' when they have finished.

God told Noah that the rainbow was a sign of the agreement he had made never to flood the earth again. God has made many promises to us in the Bible. God never breaks his promises. He always does what he says.

For younger children:
Each group will probably need a leader to help tie the wool together.

8

Tower of Babel

Genesis 11:1-9

Key verse: 'Come, let us go down and confuse their language so that they will not understand each other' (Genesis 11:7).

Theme: Sin.

Aim: To help the children remember the story of the Tower of Babel.

Preparation:

Collect together a large number of children's building blocks or Jenga bricks.

Alternatively, you could use playing cards and a packet of hula-hoops, or similar. Prepare a separate card for each team on which is written the name of a shape, different for each team.

How to play:

Form pairs or small groups and provide each with an equal number of building blocks.

Tell them that each group must pretend to be a group of engineers who must build a model of a tall tower that will be constructed in an important city. Give each group one of the pre-prepared cards.

They must build a tower in the shape described by their word, e.g. circular, square, triangular. The first team to finish their tower, using all their bricks and in the correct shape, wins.

Imagine what would have happened if all the groups had tried to work together to build one big tower. They were all trying to build different shaped towers and so it would have been impossible.

When God saw the people on earth trying to build a tall tower, he confused their languages so that they could not complete the task. The tower would have been a symbol of their power and rule over the world. God did not want people to think that they were in charge – he was the ruler, not mankind.

For younger children:
Groups can see who can build the tallest tower in a set time.

9

Off on their travels

Genesis 12:1-9

Key verse: The Lord said to Abraham, 'Leave your country, your people and your father's household and go to the land I will show you' (Genesis 12:1).

Themes: Obedience; faith.

Aim: To help the children remember Abraham's obedience when God told him to 'Go'.

Preparation:

Set up an obstacle course around your room that passes the place signs Ur, Haran, Shechem and Bethel.

How to play:

Form teams of three to represent Abram, Sarai and Lot. On the word 'Go', one person should pick up a large rucksack, one a case and one a large box. At each location sign luggage must be swapped from one person to another before continuing. Time each team to complete the course.

Abraham obeyed God and left his home. He did not know where he was going but had to trust God for the future.

For younger children:

Adjust the size of the luggage according to the size of the children, and make the obstacles easier to negotiate.

10

Good timing

Genesis 21:1-6

Key verse:　　Sarah became pregnant and bore a son to Abraham in his old age, at the very time God had promised him (Genesis 21:2).

Themes:　　God's power; families, miracles.

Aim:　　To introduce the topic of good timing. God timed the events of Abraham's life perfectly.

Preparation:

Set up a form of table tennis or short tennis.

How to play:

Line the group up, half of them on one side of the 'net' and half on the other. Once the front person has hit the ball they run round to the other side of the table or 'court' and join the back of the line there.

If the front person each time has good timing and hits the ball, a continuous rally will result. Anyone who misses is out.

Good timing is to do with being in the right place at the right time. You have to be ready and in the right place to hit the ball in a game of tennis. You need good timing to hit the ball. Abraham and Sarah had waited years for a son, but God always make sure things happen just at the right time. Isaac was born just at the right time so that he fitted into God's plans. We can trust God's good timing for our lives.

For younger children:
Younger children can roll a football between two large 'goals' marked with cones. The child at the front of the line each time catches the ball before it goes through the 'goal'. They then roll it back towards the other goal and run round to the other side to join the back of that line.

11

Boy meets girl

Genesis 24:1-67

Key verse: As for me, the Lord has led me on the journey to the house of my master's relatives (Genesis 24:27).

Theme: Guidance.

Aim: To introduce the story of how Isaac, Abraham's son, came to meet his future wife through God's guidance of Abraham's servant.

Preparation:
You will need an A4 piece of paper and a pencil for each group member. For the alternative activity, you will need a ball of string and scissors.

How to play:
To start the activity, everyone should be sitting in a circle, each with paper and pencil. A leader asks everyone to write a boy's name on the top of their piece of paper. Once it's written, each person folds the top of their paper over so that no one can see the name. Everyone then passes their paper to the right.

On the piece of paper they receive, each person then writes a girl's name, just below the fold. The papers are folded and passed on again and the process continues until each of the following has been written on each piece of paper.
• A boy's name
• A girl's name
• What sort of girl he was looking for

- What sort of guy she was looking for
- Who introduced them to each other
- Where they met
- What she thought
- What he thought
- What her father thought
- What his father thought
- The consequences (what happened in the end)

Ask group members to try to make their answers funny. At the end, the leader can collect the papers and choose the funniest ones to read out, linking them in a story based on the questions. Avoid asking the group members themselves to open and read out answers, in case of any prove to be 'unsuitable'. If you think there's a danger that your group won't participate in the light-hearted way intended, use the alternative activity below.

People get to meet each other in many different ways. Think of someone you know who is married. Do you know how they met? It can be quite funny to hear about what they thought of each other when they first met. In the story of Isaac and Rebekah, God helped a servant from Isaac's family to find the right girl for Isaac.

For younger children:
Cut lengths of string of several metres. Give each girl one end of a piece of string. Muddle up the strings so that you can't tell which string is held by which girl. Ask boys to choose a loose end of string and to gradually roll up the string, untangling it as they go, until they reach the girl at the other end. To provide an incentive, one girl could be given a bar of chocolate that she must share with whichever boy reaches her.

12

Water for the camels

Genesis 24:12-26

Key verse: As for me, the Lord has led me on the journey
to the house of my master's relatives (Genesis
24:27).

Theme: Guidance.

Aim: To reinforce the story of how God helped
Abraham's servant to know that Rebekah was
the girl for Isaac.

Preparation:

Use a large bucket of water to represent a well and several
large bowls to represent camel 'drinking troughs'. Position
the 'well' and 'drinking troughs' at opposite ends of your
room.

How to play:

Ask your group members to form pairs, boy-girl pairs if possible. One of each pair (the girl) is responsible for collecting
water from the 'well' using a plastic drinking cup or pot, held
on their shoulder like Rebekah's water jar. The other person
(the boy) pours the cup of water into their 'trough'.

Give the pairs three minutes to collect as much water as
possible for their imaginary camels. Measure the amount of
water in each 'trough' using a measuring jug and give a prize
to the winning pair.

**Abraham's servant prayed to God for help in finding the
right girl for Isaac. He did not rely on his own feelings**

but asked God to show him. God showed him a girl who was kind and helpful. He found out that she was from the family of one of Abraham's relatives so he knew she would make a suitable wife for Isaac.

For younger children:
Have a shorter distance between 'well' and 'trough'. The children could work together in one big team, filling up a trough as quickly as they can.

13

Guess who?

Genesis 25:19-34; 27:1-40
Key verse: Isaac ... loved Esau, but Rebekah loved Jacob
(Genesis 25:28).
Theme: Sin.
Aim: To help the children remember how Jacob
deceived his father by pretending to be Esau.

How to play:
One group member should be blindfolded. Meanwhile, a
leader chooses another group member to be identified by the
blindfolded player. The 'mystery' group member should
swap a piece of clothing, pair of glasses or similar with
another group member in order to make himself harder to
identify.

The leader then guides the blindfolded player and helps
them to find the shoulders, head and feet of the mystery
group member. Once they have guessed his identity, another
pair of players can be chosen.

Alternatively, have mystery guests for children to identify
drawn from your congregation, instead of other group members. Have one or two easy ones (e.g. the vicar or one of the
other leaders; someone with a beard), and a couple that the
children will know but will be more difficult.

**Rebekah helped Jacob to deceive his blind father by
disguising him as Esau, the elder of her twin boys.
From birth, Jacob and Esau had been very different in
both looks and character. Rebekah's favourite was**

Jacob, while Isaac's favourite was Esau. This caused all sorts of problems in the family. It's not right to have favourites in families or to deceive people like Rebekah and Jacob did.

For younger children:
Have several items in a drawstring bag. Invite children in turn to place a hand in the bag and feel until they can identify an object.

14

Mat Netball

Genesis 28:10-15

Key verse: I am with you and will watch over you wherever
                you go, and I will bring you back to this land. I
                will not leave you until I have done what I have
                promised (Genesis 28:15).

Theme: Promises.

Aim: To introduce the idea that God is always close to
                us.

Preparation:
This game requires two teams, a ball and two mats or hoops
placed at opposite ends of the room.

How to play:
One person from each team acts as the 'goal' and must
remain standing on the mat or in the hoop throughout the
game. The aim of each team is to throw the ball so that their
'goal' can catch it. No one is allowed to run with the ball, or
kick it, or bounce it like a basketball.

Each team member must find a member of the opposite
team to 'mark', as in netball. Try to pair up people of approximately equal height. When marking, players stay as close to
their partner as possible without touching them.

**In this game, you try to get away from the person mark-
ing you, but, if they play well, they will always be close
to you. Jacob found out that God was always close to
him (Genesis 28:15). God is always close to us too.**

Unlike the partner who is marking us, we shouldn't try to get away from God! God is a very helpful and essential partner, not one who gets in the way.

For younger children:
Form pairs of children. Ask one child to try to run away from the other while their partner stays as close to them as possible, trying to be like their shadow. After a short time they can swap roles.

15

I'm the best!

Genesis 37:1-28

Key verse: When his brothers saw that their father loved
him more than any of them, they hated him and
could not speak a kind word to him (Genesis
37:4).

Theme: Sin.

Aim: To introduce the topic of jealousy.

Preparation:

This game involves shooting at various targets, so you will
need to set up, for example, a basketball net (or leader holding a bin); a football goal with a leader to be goal keeper; a
child's dart board.

How to play:

Firstly, each child is given a turn at trying to score a basket
from a marked line. Make it fairly difficult but not impossible. Give each child three attempts. Keep score.

Secondly, each child is given a turn at trying to score a
goal passed the goalkeeper in the football goal. Again, make
it fairly difficult but not impossible. Give each child three
attempts. Keep score.

Lastly, each child is given a turn at trying to score as many
points as possible on the dart board. Give each child three
attempts. Keep score. See who has the highest score.

Once the children have all had three turns at each activity, a leader is given three attempts at each and boasts that he
will definitely beat their scores. He is the best! For the bas-

ketball shooting, he is allowed to stand on a chair, or the leader holding the bin moves the bin to make it easy to score.

For the football shooting, the goalkeeper will not save any of the goals. For the darts, the leader stands very close. Of course, the leader will have the winning score and the children will complain loudly that it isn't fair!

Allow them to suggest ways of making each activity harder for the leader instead of easier and let him try again.

It's easy to feel cross when something seems unfair, or jealous when someone else is doing better than you are. Joseph's brothers were jealous of him because he was their father's favourite.

What made it worse was he boasted to them about dreams where they all bowed down to him. Joseph shouldn't have shown off to them, and his father shouldn't have made him his favourite, but it was not right that his brothers felt so jealous and wanted to get rid of him.

Do you ever make people jealous of you? What should you do if you feel jealous of someone else?

For younger children:
Adjust the shooting activities as appropriate.

16

Burdened

Genesis 45:1-18

Key verse: 'And now, do not be distressed and do not be angry with yourselves for selling me here, because it was to save lives that God sent me ahead of you' (Genesis 45:5).

Theme: Forgiveness.

Aim: To help the children to understand that it is hard to have good relationships and get on well in life if you hold on to bad feelings like anger, hate and worry.

Preparation:
Label two sets of shoe boxes, or similar, with words such as these: bitterness, hate, grudge, anger, fear, worry, spite, hostility, rage, fury, anxiety. You will also need a football for each team.

How to play:
Firstly, briefly discuss the meanings of the words and talk about what may cause someone to have these feelings.

Next, divide the group into teams of three or more. Two in each team should gently pass a football to each other, rolling it using their feet, or, if you want to make the game harder, catching it. If you don't have much space, they need only be a few metres apart and teams could take it in turns to play.

The other team member(s) then pass boxes, one at a time, to one of the ball-passing team members. They have to try and hold onto all the boxes they are given while continuing to pass the ball. They must successfully pass the ball five times before taking another box.

As they are given more boxes, they will start to find it very difficult or impossible to pass the ball without dropping boxes. Count how many boxes they manage to hold while still passing the ball. The winner is the person holding most boxes while still able to pass the ball five times.

It was difficult to carry on passing the ball while holding lots of boxes. If we're holding some of these negative feelings inside us, for whatever reason, it is hard to get on well with others.

People will find us hard to get to know and we may have trouble making good friends. We need to get rid of these feelings. Forgiveness is part of that process – Joseph forgave his brothers so that they could be friends.

For younger children:

Ask two children each to hold one end of two skipping ropes. These children will act as 'anchors'. They stand still, ideally about ten metres apart, and hold tightly to their end of rope. Ask two other children to be their partners and to hold the other ends. These children are the 'players' and should stand facing each other, close to their partners.

The players then gently kick a ball to each other. Depending on their ball kicking ability, it will sometimes be impossible for them to reach the ball while still holding the rope. Allow other pairs of children to have a turn.

You can explain that like it's hard to play well while holding the rope, if we hold on to cross or bad feelings about people it's hard to get on well in life.

17

Matching pairs

Exodus 1:6 – 2:10

Key verse: She named him Moses, saying, 'I drew him out of the water' (Exodus 2:10).

Theme: Families.

Aim: To help children understand that God has plans for our lives but we may not always understand what he is doing. God sees 'the big picture' so we can trust him.

Preparation:

Hide two or three sets of the following items around your room: shoe and lace; cup and saucer; torch and battery; pen and lid; book and cover; glasses and case; two pieces from a jigsaw.

You will also need the rest of the jigsaw pieces later. Write and photocopy a list so that the children will know what they are looking for.

How to play:

Form two or three teams and give each a list of hidden items. Give teams several minutes to find the items, collect them in their team's area and put them into pairs.

These things all belong together. We belong in families. God has given us to each other. God gave Moses two families. First he had his Mum, Dad and sister and then he was adopted as part of the Pharaoh's family.

Look at the jigsaw pieces together and provide the rest of the pieces so that team can complete their pictures.

When we just had a few pieces of the puzzle we couldn't see what the picture was going to be. Life was a bit like that for Moses. He didn't know why he had been rescued from the river and adopted by the Pharaoh's daughter. He only had the first few pieces of his life. But God had a big plan for him and gradually he understood more.

You just have the first few pieces of your life but God has all the other pieces and you can trust him with his plan for you.

For younger children:
Have children all work together to find the items and bring them to you.

18

Guess the plague

Exodus 7:14 – 10:29

Key verse: Then the Lord said to Moses, 'Pharaoh's heart is unyielding; he refuses to let the people go (Exodus 7:14).

Theme: Miracles.

Aim: To help the children to remember the first nine of the plagues of Egypt.

Preparation:

You will need a large number of bits and pieces for these activities, but it will be worth the effort!

Here's a list of things to gather together: four blindfolds; tomato soup in bowls with spoons; pickled gherkins; a pot of hundreds and thousands; two cups of raisins and a fly-swatter or rolled up newspaper for each person.

Then you'll also need some wafer-thin pastrami; several jam doughnuts plus one custard-filled one; knitting needles; two bags of ice cubes and a bucket; rice crispies and two clean trays.

How to play:

If you have a large group, choose a few people for each activity so that everyone has at least one turn.

For the first four plagues, blindfold four volunteers and have a food tasting competition. Check for food allergies before you begin. The volunteers must guess which plague is represented by what they are eating:

River of blood: Lukewarm tomato soup

Frogs: Pickled gherkins cut in the shape of frogs' legs

Gnats: A few 'hundreds and thousands', which will be small and crunchy

Livestock: Wafer-thin pastrami

For the next plagues you will need two teams.

Flies: Provide each team with fly swatters or rolled up newspapers and a cup of raisins. One team throws raisins at the opposition (each person may only throw one at a time). The opposition tries to swat the 'flies' away. Any flies landing in the opposition's area count against them. Reverse roles for round two.

Boils: You will need a bowl of five jam doughnuts plus one custard doughnut. Selected volunteers from two teams take turns at plunging knitting needles into the bowl. Needles emerging clean score no points. Needles with jam (blood) score 5 points. Needles with custard (pus from the boil) score 20 points. Whatever happens, the 'boils' get lanced. Disgusting but fun!

Hail: Provide each team with a bag of ice cubes. Place a bucket at the other end of the room. Teams attempt to throw ice cubes into the bucket – 10 points for cubes on target.

Locusts: Give each team a tray on which a trail of rice crispies is set out. A volunteer from each team must race to devour their trail of cereal, locust-like, with no hands.

Darkness: Blindfold two volunteers from each team and stand them in the four corners of the room. On the word 'go' they must find the other volunteer from their team as quickly as possible. Add a few soft obstacles to make it harder.

The rest of the team may shout directions, which the volunteers will probably find totally confusing!

There were nine plagues before the final plague, the plague on the firstborn. Moses must have felt very frustrated as time went by. Whatever happened, Pharaoh still would not let the people go. Sometimes we have to wait a long time for God to do what he says.

For younger children:
Stick to tasting all the different foods, in the order in which the plagues came (tomato soup; pickled gherkins; 'hundreds and thousands; raisins; wafer-thin pastrami; doughnuts; small pieces of ice or ice lollies; rice crispies) and telling the children which plague each represents. For the plague of darkness, choose someone brave enough to taste an unknown food whilst blindfolded.

19

Passover Relay

Exodus 12:1-42

Key verse: This is how you are to eat it: with your cloak
                tucked into your belt, your sandals on your feet
                and your staff in your hand. Eat it in haste; it is
                the Lord's Passover (Exodus 12:11).

Theme: Obedience.

Aim: To help the children remember the events of the
                Passover.

Preparation:

For each team, you will need a 'cloak', a belt, a pair of sandals,
a staff and a plate of pitta bread and lamb paste.

How to play:

This game is based on the things the Israelites were told to
do on Passover night (Exodus 12:8-11). Form two or more
teams. In relay style, each team member must run to the
other end of the room where they will find a cloak, a belt,
and sandals to put on, and a staff and plate of pitta bread
with lamb paste for them to hold. They then run back
around their team and then back to where they found the
clothes. Here, they exchange them with the next person in
their team. First team to finish wins a pile of gold chocolate
coins.

**The Israelites obeyed God's instructions and prepared
themselves to leave Egypt. God knew that the
Egyptians would urge them to hurry out of their**

country when the last plague came. The final plague was so terrible that Pharaoh summoned Moses and Aaron during the night to tell them to leave.

For younger children:
Have just one team member dress up. Send other team members, relay style, to collect the clothes etc. for them. Have a leader available to help each child who is dressing up.

20

First to Ten

Exodus 20:3-17

Key verse: You shall have no other gods before me (Exodus 20:3).

Theme: Obedience.

Aim: To help the children to remember and apply the Ten Commandments.

Preparation:

Pin up numbers 1-10 around the room. You will need to provide Bibles or lists of the Ten Commandments, one between two.

How to play:

Divide into teams. Read out a short description of someone breaking a commandment.

Using Bibles or a list of the Ten Commandments, each team must decide which commandment is being broken, and which number it is. They then send someone to stand by that number. The first person to reach the right number scores a point.

If more than one commandment is being broken, the team must send two or more people to the correct numbers. First team to gain ten points wins.

Example commandment breaking descriptions:

- Luke was arrested for theft (8).
- Mary's got a habit of saying 'Oh my God' (3).
- Sanjay was talking in class, but told the teacher it wasn't

him but Reece who was talking (9).

• The newspaper report said that someone had been shot dead during a robbery (6 & 8).

• Chloe was rude to her mum (5).

• Kerry practically worships Gareth Gates [or other current pop idol] and desperately wants a jacket like his (1 & 10).

• The male lead in the show ran off with the leading lady, but she was already married to someone else (7).

• Neil chooses to work on Sundays because he gets more money that way (2 & 4).

• Richard stole money from his mum to pay for a tarot card reading, and told his mum his brother had taken the money (8, 5, 9, 2).

God has given us instructions telling us the best way to live. He made us and so he knows! Lots of people will try to give you different advice but God's guidelines are the best ones to remember and follow.

For younger children:
Write each commandment in simple language and place a picture beside each one to help children to identify it. Display the commandments around the room. Call out very simple actions, such as 'Luke stole some sweets'. The children can run to commandments as a group rather than competing in teams.

21

Contamination

Leviticus 11:45

Key verse: I am the Lord who brought you up out of Egypt
to be your God; therefore be holy, because I am
holy (Leviticus 11:45).

Themes: Holiness; sin; obedience.

Aim: To help the children understand the concept of
holiness.

Preparation:

Prepare numbered plastic pots containing substances such as
the following: sand, water, white paint, sugar, flour, coffee. In
each pot there should also be a hidden substance which is
not immediately obvious, e.g. small pebbles in the sand, salt
dissolved in the water, a blob of black paint at the bottom of
the white, pepper in the sugar, cocoa in the flour, tea in the
coffee.

How to play:

Hold a competition where individuals take turns in examining
the pots and guessing the contents. Tell them that there is
one main substance but it may be contaminated by another
one that shouldn't be there.

Allow them to mix the substances around but not pour
them out or taste them.

Once everyone has had a go, ask for their answers and
reveal the real contents.

The sand, water, white paint, sugar, flour and coffee all contained other substances that shouldn't have been there. They were contaminated, spoilt by something. The sand was made 'lumpy' by the stones, the water was made salty by the salt, the white paint, sugar and flour all lost their pure white colour and the coffee would have tasted odd with tea in it. It would be hard to remove the contaminating substance.

God wanted his people to be a pure and holy people, specially dedicated to him. To be pure and holy means not to be contaminated by sin. If we do things that God doesn't like, we can't be pure and holy, as God wants. We can't make ourselves holy again, but God can.

For younger children:
Remove the competitive element. Pass round the pots and allow the children to mix the contents. Talk together about the contents of each pot.

22

Spy mission

Numbers 13:1-14:31; Joshua 2:1-24

Key verse: Then Caleb silenced the people before Moses
                and said, 'We should go up and take possession
                of the land, for we can certainly do it' (Numbers
                13:30).

Theme: Obedience.

Aim: To remind the children of either of the two stories
                regarding spying out the Promised Land.

Preparation:

Prepare the mission envelopes, as detailed below.

How to play:

This activity will require your whole group and will work best
with three or more groups of four or more young people. If
your group is small, divide into two or more pairs and adapt
the instructions as required.

Each group must sit in a different corner of the room and
be given a sealed envelope containing their mission. On the
word 'Go' they open the envelope and quietly read the
instructions, ensuring no other group hears what they have
to do. They should then carry out the instructions as quickly
as possible. Example 'missions':

• Each member of your group, in turn, must go outside,
collect a small stone, and bring it back.

• Each member of your group, in turn, must go and wash
their hands and then return.

• Each member of your group, in turn, must remove one

shoe, throw it in the air and catch it three times, and then replace it.

• Each member of your group, in turn, must collect the signature of a leader (it does not have to be a different leader each time) on this envelope.

They must finish within five minutes. The catch is that while carrying out their mission, each team must try to discover the mission of the other teams. They will therefore also need to try to conceal what they are doing from other teams to prevent them from finding out their mission.

Fifty points should be awarded for teams finishing within the time limit, whilst twenty points should be awarded for each of the other team's missions that have been guessed by each team.

Moses sent a leader from each tribe to go to explore the Promised Land. Some saw things one way and were afraid whilst two of them, Joshua and Caleb, saw things very differently, through God's eyes. But the people were too afraid to take the land. As a result they spent 40 years wandering in the wilderness. When that generation had died and Joshua had become their new leader, spies were again sent out. This time the Israelites went forward into the land.

For younger children:
Tell your children that they are going to pretend to be spies. To be a good spy you have to be able to look at things very carefully. Ask them all to have a good look at your room. Then take them out, or ask them to turn round and close their eyes, and make a few small changes. Children who spot the changes will be awarded points. Repeat several times and see who is your champion spy.

23

Key Commands

Deuteronomy 5:1-22; 11:1,8

Key verse: Love the Lord your God and keep his require-
ments, his decrees, his laws and his commands
always (Deuteronomy 11:1).

Themes: Obedience; holiness; sin.

Aim: To help the children to remember and understand the Ten Commandments.

Preparation:

On small pieces of paper write down either one of the commandments or another common saying. Place each piece of
paper inside a balloon and inflate it.

    Ideas for common sayings:

- Choose the lesser of two evils.
- Don't throw the baby out with the bath water.
- Don't cut off the bough you're standing on.
- Don't count your chickens before they've hatched
- Do as I say, not as I do.
- Don't teach your grandmother to suck eggs.
- Look before you leap.

    You will also need two buckets for each team, one labelled
'Key Commands' and the other, 'Simply sayings'.

How to play:

Divide the group into two or more teams and place the
balloons at the other end of the room. Teams run in relay
style to fetch the balloons one at a time. Each balloon should
then be burst, the instruction read and then placed in the cor-

rect bucket. At the end, count up their correct answers. The team with the most answers correct wins. (Be ready to explain the meaning of some of the sayings.)

Moses reminded the Israelites of God's commandments as they were on the brink of entering the Promised Land.
We need reminding of God's commandments too, as we hear all sorts of other instructions and pieces of advice in everyday life. We need to remember that God's advice is best.

For younger children:
In larger writing on larger pieces of paper write the commandments in simple language and other simple pieces of bad advice such as 'Eat lots of sweets'. Hide the pieces of paper around the room.

Label two buckets 'God's Key Commands' and 'Don't listen to this!' and have a helper stationed beside each.

Children search for the pieces of paper and, when they find one, run to a helper who will help them to read the instruction and decide in which bucket to place it.

24

Round and round and round...

Joshua 6:1-20 Jericho

Key verse: The seventh time around, when the priests sounded the trumpet blast, Joshua commanded the people, 'Shout! For the Lord has given you the city!' (Joshua 6:16)

Theme: Obedience.

Aim: To help the children remember the story of the fall of Jericho.

Preparation:

Place some tables, chairs or boxes in the middle of the room to represent Jericho. You will also need a large box with two broom handles pushed through it to represent the ark, some type of 'trumpet', and either some raw eggs or a plastic jug of water.

How to play:

Form two or more teams. Time the teams, one at a time, as they circle 'Jericho' while some carry a large box to represent the ark and others blow some type of 'trumpet'. Place either some raw eggs or a cup of water on top of the box so that they have to be very careful with it, as the Israelites had to be careful with the ark. Broken eggs or spilt water will result in time penalties, e.g. twenty seconds added for each broken egg or 50ml of water lost.

Each team should circle 'Jericho' six times, stopping at a set point each time and lowering the ark to the floor to signify night at the camp, and then seven times without stopping, as the Israelites did on the seventh day (Joshua 6: 2-5). To stop the clock, as they finish they must yell at the top of their voices.

The Israelites, under Joshua, obeyed God and he gave them the city of Jericho as he had promised.

The method of victory was certainly unusual, but God doesn't always do things as we expect.

For younger children:
Place a Bible in the 'ark'. Choose four children to carry the 'ark' and line others up behind with instruments. Play a song such as 'The Lord's Army' and have the whole group march round 'Jericho' seven times while singing and playing.

25

I can't do that!

Judges 6

Key verse: 'But Lord,' Gideon asked, 'how can I save Israel?
                 My clan is the weakest in Manasseh, and I am the
                 least in my family' (Judges 6: 15).

Theme: Self-image.

Aim: To think about our feelings of inadequacy, prior
                 to learning about Gideon and how God can
                 overcome our weaknesses.

Preparation:
You will need several chairs, a volunteer leader and a list such
as that below.

How to play:
This game involves the children guessing what a leader is and
isn't good at. Read out the following activities one by one:
• Singing a solo
• Painting a self-portrait
• Playing centre forward in a football match
• Making a cake
• Running in the local fun run
• Entertaining a two year old for an hour
• Typing a letter on the computer
• Going swimming with an international swimmer
• Entering a talent competition
• Going ice-skating

If they would think the leader would feel quite confident at
performing the activity, they should stand on a chair. If they

think they would like to avoid it because it would make them feel 'not good enough', they should run to a corner of the room. If they would think the leader would feel just 'OK' about it, they should sit on the floor.

After each activity has been read out and the children have decided what they think, the leader can reveal their answer. Children in the correct place win points.

Sometimes we feel inadequate, perhaps particularly when we feel we're not that good at something compared with other people. We don't like to feel inferior. Often we will try to back out or make excuses if we're asked to do something that we don't think we are much good at. Gideon felt inadequate for the task God had chosen him to do.

For younger children:
Ask the children to stand on the 'Yes' or 'No' side of a line marked on the floor depending on whether they think a leader can or can't do what you call out. For example: Can you sing 'Humpty Dumpty?' 'Can you do a forward roll?' 'Can you swim ten lengths without stopping?'

26

Strength Challenge

Judges 16

Key verse: 'If my head were shaved, my strength would leave me and I would become as weak as any other man' (Judges 16:17).

Themes: Holiness, obedience; miracles.

Aim: To introduce the topic of strength and reliance on God.

Preparation:

You will need several newspapers, some bathroom scales and a ball of thin wool.

How to play:

Challenge children to undertake one or more of these strength challenges:

• Paper tearing – How many sheets of newspaper can you tear through?

• Leg push – Stand the bathroom scales almost vertically against a wall in a corridor. Participants sit with their back against the opposite wall and feet against the scales. They push against the scales for five seconds and see what weight they can achieve. (If you don't have a narrow enough corridor, you may need to place a strong, solid object, or a few bricks, behind the scales so that the children can reach them.)

• Wool snapping – How many strands of wool can you snap at once by pulling? (Watch out – some children may cut their fingers if they try too hard.)

• Arm wrestling and Tug of War competitions are further

options. Please be careful: try to ensure the contestants are reasonably equal in strength; and don't ask children to lift heavy objects as part of a strength challenge since they may injure themselves.

The strength of our muscles determines how strong we are. Some people are stronger than others. Some adults do special training to make themselves strong for weight lifting competitions. Samson was a man who was even stronger than these people because he had a special strength from God.

For younger children:
Paper tearing will be the simplest option.

27

Find a Family

1 Samuel 1:1-28

Key verse: 'I prayed for this child, and the Lord has grant-
ed me what I asked of him.' (1 Samuel 1:27).

Themes: Families; prayer.

Aim: To introduce the theme of families, prior to
reading about Hannah and her family.

Preparation:

Collect together a selection of men's shirts, skirts, baggy T-
shirts, men's and ladies' hats and shoes, bobble hats and
wellington boots.

How to play:

Divide your group into teams of three and set them off on
a relay where one person must dress up as 'Mum', one as
'Dad' and one as 'Junior'. In total, each person will run to the
other end of the course three times.

'Dad' must pick up and put on a shirt the first time, then
shoes, then a hat. 'Mum' should do the same but putting on
a skirt first. 'Junior' should put on a T-shirt, bobble hat and
wellies. Make sure the clothes that you provide are all big
enough for the largest member of your group, and preferably
big enough for a leader in case you need to make up the numbers in a team.

**Not everyone has Mum, Dad and children in their
family. Not all kids have both Mum and Dad, not
everyone has a husband or wife and not all couples have**

children. Hannah was a lady who was married but did not have children. She longed and prayed for a baby but to start with it seemed God was not going to give her a child.

Sometimes people have hard times in their families, but God is still there to help us.

For younger children:
For each child, you will need a piece of paper with the name 'Father', 'Mother' or 'Junior' plus an animal name or picture (you could use animal Happy Family cards). Give everyone an animal card. The aim of the game is for everyone to find the other members of their family by either making the noise of their animal or miming the movement of their animal.

For example, Father Duck, Mother Duck and Duck Junior should all 'quack' or waddle about. The 'family' should sit down in a group of three when they have found each other.

28

Sound bites

1 Samuel 3:1-21 Samuel

Key verse: The Lord came and stood there, calling as at the other times, 'Samuel! Samuel!' Then Samuel said, 'Speak, for your servant is listening' (1 Samuel 3:10).

Theme: Prayer.

Aim: To introduce the theme of listening to God.

Preparation:

Record short snippets of celebrity voices from the television or radio. Stick up the pictures (or write up the names) of the celebrities around the room for children to run to when they hear their voices.

How to play:

Ask the children to stand in the middle of the room. Play the tape, stopping after each voice to allow the children to run to the appropriate picture or name.

Give a point to each child who guesses correctly.

We have to listen carefully in order to guess the voices. Samuel, when he was a little boy, learned to listen carefully and hear God speaking to him.

For younger children:

Record a series of sounds for the children to try to identify, instead of voices, or make the sounds 'live', unobserved. Bring an object that represents each sound to your session, e.g. a jug representing the sound of water being poured into a beaker; a roll of sticky tape representing a parcel being wrapped; a packet of cereal representing crunchy cereal being eaten; a key representing a door being unlocked.

Place the objects on sheets of brightly coloured card around the edges of your room.

29

Inside Out

1 Samuel 16:1-13

Key verse: 'The Lord does not look at the things man looks at. Man looks at the outward appearance, but the Lord looks at the heart' (1 Samuel 16:7).

Theme: Self-image.

Aim: To emphasize that while people tend to be concerned with outside appearances, God is more concerned with what a person is like inside.

Preparation:

You will need a selection of empty food containers and boxes such as margarine tubs, chocolate boxes, cereal boxes, etc. You will need at least one per child. Prior to re-sealing the containers, place some sweets inside the less exciting looking containers and some cold cooked brussel spouts or similar inside the more attractive looking ones. Check for food allergies.

How to play:

Display the food containers and boxes. Children must come up one at a time and choose one container (without picking it up and shaking it first!). They then take it back to their place. Some will go for a chocolate box, expecting to find chocolate inside. Others may have done this sort of thing before and might go for the margarine tub. Once everyone has chosen, allow each person to open their container and eat what they find. This activity could be done as a relay race. Teams share the contents of their containers.

Food containers normally contain what they say they contain. But we couldn't tell what was in the containers we've just chosen. You might have chosen a chocolate box because you like chocolates but you couldn't see what was inside. We sometimes look at people on the outside and decide what they are like by what they look like.

But when God looks at people, he is most interested on what they are like inside not outside. He looks at the heart not the outward appearance.

For younger children:
Without the relay race option, this activity will be fine for most ages.

30

Giant Slaying

1 Samuel 17:1-58

Key verse: David said to the Philistine, 'You come against me with sword and spear and javelin, but I come against you in the name of the Lord Almighty, the God of the armies of Israel, whom you have defied' (1 Samuel 17:45).

Theme: Miracles.

Aim: To help the children remember how David overcame Goliath with God's help.

Preparation:

Draw and cut out an outline of a huge nine-foot-high man (1.5 metres) and stick it to a wall in your room. You will also need a box of tissues and a bowl of water. You may like to cover the floor under 'Goliath' with a plastic sheet, to protect the floorcovering from the shots that fall short.

How to play:

Form two or more teams. Children take it in turns to make a wet ball of tissue and aim it at Goliath's head. Award points depending on where they hit him and whether the tissue sticks: 20 points if the tissue sticks to his head, 10 points if it hits and falls off. 5 points if it sticks to another part of his body. No points at all if they miss.

Goliath was bigger and stronger and more experienced at fighting than David. However, David had killed wild animals while caring for his father's sheep and he knew

that with God's help he could defeat this enemy of God's people. God can also help us when we face frightening things.

For younger children:
You may like to make Goliath a bit smaller or allow children to stand on a chair to throw (making sure they don't throw themselves off the chair as they throw their missile!)

31

Protect the hem

1 Samuel 24:1-22

Key verse: 'When a man finds his enemy does he let him get away unharmed? May the Lord reward you well for the way you treated me today' (1 Samuel 24:19).

Theme: Forgiveness.

Aim: To help the children remember the story of how David had the opportunity to creep up on Saul and kill him – whereas instead he just took a small piece of his robe.

Preparation:

You will need a handkerchief, a blindfold and several cups of water. You will also need a mop to clear up afterwards if you play indoors.

How to play:

It is best to play this game outdoors due to the amount of water involved.

Sit or stand in a circle with a blindfolded volunteer, 'Saul', standing in the middle, armed with a plastic cup filled with water. Saul must tuck a handkerchief into his waistband, leaving at least 75% of the material hanging out over one hip. He listens for people creeping up to him.

In turn, group members from the circle are given the chance to try to grab the handkerchief and take it back to his or her place without being soaked by Saul.

Anyone who succeeds gets a turn in the middle.

David had the chance to get his revenge on Saul. One day he had the chance to kill Saul but instead just crept up to him and cut off a piece of his robe without Saul realising. David was determined not to repay evil with evil. God wants us to treat people well even if they do something to harm us.

For younger children:
Sit in a circle with a leader standing in the middle blind-folded. Place a bunch of keys, or if you can play outside, a plastic cup full of water, beside him or her. Children sitting in the circle take it in turns to silently walk and grab the keys/cup.

The blindfolded leader must try to touch the other child before the child can grab the keys/cup and return to their place.

Children who grab the keys/cup and return to their place without being caught win a point.

32

Share the Plunder

1 Samuel 30:1-25

Key verse: 'The share of the man who stayed with the supplies is to be the same as that of him who went down to battle. All shall share alike' (1 Samuel 30:24).

Theme: Sharing.

Aim: To reinforce the story of how David promoted unity amongst his men.

Preparation:
You will need plenty of biscuits. Check for allergies.

How to play:
Divide into two or more teams and run a relay where team members must run (or hop or crawl) to the other end of the room, collect a biscuit from a central pile and return. Teams must pick only two or three team members to run, while the others stay behind and cheer them on.

Continue for a set time, or until all the biscuits have been taken. The biscuits must then be shared equally within each team.

In David's army, those with enough energy carried on to fight the battle, but those who were exhausted were allowed to stay behind. When those who had been fighting returned, they shared the plunder with those who had stayed behind.

David knew that all his men were important so he wanted everyone to share together. He wanted the whole army to feel united, and to avoid gangs or cliques amongst his men.

In the church, people have different roles and some people look as though they are doing more than others are. The important thing is that everyone does their best for God and that we all work together for him, in unity.

For younger children:
Emphasize the sharing aspect of the story. Instead of a relay you could ask each child to choose from a selection of containers in which are hidden a varying number of sweets. Once everyone has chosen, children share the sweets out equally.

33

Approach with caution

2 Samuel 6:1-15

Key verse: David was afraid of the Lord that day and said, 'How can the ark of God ever come to me?' (2 Samuel 6:9)

Theme: Holiness.

Aim: To introduce the story of Uzzah and the ark of God. Also, to introduce the idea that, through Jesus, we can approach God with confidence (Hebrews 4:14-16).

Preparation:

Write actions such as those below on separate pieces of card.

- Approaching a large bonfire
- Approaching a boisterous dog
- Approaching a cold shower
- Approaching a nervous kitten
- Approaching a sleeping baby
- Approaching a huge mansion
- Approaching your mum
- Approaching your best friend's house
- Approaching the edge of a cliff
- Approaching a crying child

How to play:

Choose a volunteer who will be given one of the above actions to mime to the rest of the group. Tell the group that all the actions involve approaching something or someone and they have to guess what or who is being approached.

Once someone guesses the first action, they then mime the next one.

If you have a large group, divide into smaller groups for this activity. To make it competitive, challenge groups to guess all ten as quickly as possible and provide a prize for the winning team.

What you know about something and how you feel about it affects how you approach it. Some things, such as large dogs, may appear a bit scary at first, but once you get to know them they might be quite friendly. Edges of cliffs are always dangerous. Crying children normally require kindness and sympathy.

Today we're going to think about how people approach God. Some people think he doesn't exist, so don't bother approaching at all. Some people are scared of him and keep their distance. Other people treat him like a friend and relate to him confidently, but still with respect, reverence and awe.

For younger children:
Ask all the children to mime each action together. Choose one or two children who are miming particularly well to show the rest of the group.

34

Solomon's Temple

1 Kings 5:1-7; 8:22-30

Key verse: I intend, therefore, to build a temple for the Name of the Lord my God, as the Lord told my father David when he said, 'Your son whom I will put on the throne in your place will build the temple for my name' (1 Kings 5:5).

Theme: The temple.

Aim: To help the children learn more about the temple that Solomon built.

Preparation:

For each team you will need a large die and items to represent the following parts of the temple: the portico (porch area), the Holy Place, the Most Holy Place, the altar, five lampstands, five more lampstands, and the ark of the covenant.

Large pieces of card cut to the appropriate sizes, labelled and laid flat on the floor can represent the three areas; children's building blocks can be used for the other items.

You will need a diagram of Solomon's temple to help you with the layout. Before you start, show the children how to lay out a plan of Solomon's temple using the props.

How to play:

Teams of four to six children sit in a circle and take it in turns to roll a die.

When someone rolls a '1', they may run to the middle of the room and find the 'portico'. They bring this back to the middle of the team. When someone rolls a '2', they may run to the middle of the room and find the 'Holy Place'. They bring this back to the middle of the team. The game continues in the same way with '3' needed for the 'Most Holy Place', '4' for the 'altar', '5' for the first five lampstands, and another '5' for the other five lampstands, and a '6' for the 'ark of the covenant'. The parts of the temple can be collected in any order, except the ark must be collected last, i.e. rolling a six is no good until all the other parts are in place. The die must be passed to the next player if the matching part has already been collected.

Solomon built a magnificent temple for God. We have made a plan to give us an idea of what it was like. It had three parts to it. The walls were made of wood covered with gold. The floors were also covered with gold. There were carvings of trees and flowers. There were two bronze pillars at the front. As well as the golden lampstands, the gold altar and the Ark of the Covenant there were many other golden items. The Ark of the Covenant was a symbol of the presence of God, but although the temple was so amazing, and God could be met there in a special way, Solomon knew that God wouldn't actually live in it like a person would. God is everywhere, not just in one place.

For younger children:
Remove the competitive element. Work together in a big circle to make a plan of the temple.

35

The Weakest Link

1 Kings 9:1-7; 11:1-13

Key verse: As Solomon grew old, his wives turned his heart after other gods, and his heart was not fully devoted to the Lord his God, as the heart of David his father had been (1 Kings 11:4).

Themes: Temptation; sin.

Aim: To introduce the idea that everyone has areas of weakness and temptation in their lives and that Jesus can help us with these.

Preparation:

For each small group or pair you will need an equally sized sheet of newspaper and ten small pieces of sticky tape.

How to play:

Each group or pair must make the strongest paper chain they can using the sheet of newspaper and sticky tape. There must be ten 'links' in the chain, but they can decide the length and width of the 'links'.

When they have finished, test each paper chain by hanging weights of increasing mass onto the bottom of each suspended chain. A plastic bag tied to the bottom 'link' to which child's bricks can be added would do.

At some stage each chain will break at its weakest point.

Provide a prize for the team with the strongest paper chain.

Which chain was the strongest? Which link broke in your chain? Can you think of a weak point in your own life – something you're not very good at or a temptation you easily give in to? Although King Solomon started out as a good and wise king, in the end he gave in to temptation and did not continue to follow the Lord with all his heart.

If you give in to temptation in just one part of your life, you will not be able to follow the Lord to the best of your ability. We need Jesus to help us in all parts of our lives, especially the parts where we are weak.

For younger children:

All the children can help to make one long paper chain. See where the chain breaks when you pull. Tell the children that you can imagine each link is like a part of life – at home with family, at school with classmates, at clubs with friends, at church with God's family, etc.

They can ask God to help them to be strong so that they can follow him in all these places. We all have to try not to be weak and not to give in to temptation.

36

Hot and bothered

1 Kings 16:29-33; 17:1

Key verse: Ahab also made an Asherah pole and did more
to provoke the Lord, the God of Israel, to
anger than did all the kings of Israel before him
(1 Kings 16:33).

Theme: Anger.

Aim: To introduce the topic of anger — what things
make us angry, and what makes God angry?

Preparation:

Write or fasten the temperatures 0°C, 10°C, 20°C ... 100°C,
evenly spaced, down the middle of the floor.

How to play:

A leader will read out situations such as those listed below
and group members must individually decide which temperature represents their feelings each time. 0°C represents '
doesn't bother me' whereas 100°C, represents 'makes me feel
very angry and hot and bothered'.

Situations:

• The cheese in your packed lunch appears to have gone
off.

• Your teacher has given you maths homework on the
wrong night.

• The price of petrol has gone up again.

• Your Mum forgot to wash your PE kit.

• Most of your friends seem to take no notice of how God
wants people to live.

- Your favourite clothes shop has closed down.
- The people who made your trainers may not have received a fair wage.
- People in some countries are dying due to lack of food, water and basic medicines.
- In some places most girls can't go to school.
- In some countries there are Christians imprisoned unjustly.

We can often be more upset about small things 'close to home' than huge injustices and evils that seem far away. We are probably more likely to complain about things that directly affect us, such as gone-off food, or other things that inconvenience us, than problems that seem too far away or too big to do anything about. But God cares greatly about these big problems. Today we're going to find out about someone who was called by God to speak out an unpopular message about the problems of a whole country.

For younger children:
Instead of running up and down a thermometer, have the children run to a wall labelled 'hot and bothered' or the opposite wall labelled 'cool and calm'. Adapt the statements to fit the age group, using simple language.

37

Time to choose

1 Kings 18

Key verse: Elijah went before the people and said, 'How long will you waver between two opinions? If the Lord is God, follow him; but if Baal is God, follow him' (1 Kings 18:21).

Themes: Love; faith.

Aim: To introduce the topic of choices.

Preparation:

Mark a central line down your room. Prepare a list of choices such as those below:

- A Chinese take away or fish and chips?
- Coke or Fanta?
- Baked beans or peas?
- A skiing holiday or a beach holiday?
- Nike or Adidas?
- Pet cat or dog?
- Tickets for a football match or a TV show?
- Coronation Street or Neighbours?
- Arsenal or Man U?
- Prayer or Astrology?

Add more examples of your own.

How to play:

Position two leaders as far from each other as possible, either side of the line. Ask your group to stand along the line. Leaders call out the different choices. Each person responds and moves to one side or the other, returning to the line after each choice. Those not able to decide, or wanting both or neither option, can stay on the line.

Sometimes it's hard to choose and we can't decide. God wants us to make up our minds about him. Some people want a little of one religion and a little of another. Our God is the only true God, so he wants us to choose to love him, and only him.

For younger children:
Adapt the choices to suit the age group. Use visual aids such as toys, breakfast cereal boxes, pictures, etc. to show the two choices each time.

38

Skipping rhyme

1 Kings 19:19-21

Key verse: So Elisha ...set out to follow Elijah and became his attendant (1 Kings 19:21).

Theme: Discipleship.

Aim: To reinforce the idea of discipleship — how one person can teach another about God, as Elijah taught Elisha to serve God as a prophet.

Preparation:
You will need a rope at least 4m long and two helpers.

How to play:
Have two helpers turn the rope. Show how to run into the rope and skip. Children who can already do it can encourage others to try and not be afraid of the rope. Learning to run in and skip without tripping over the rope takes practice.

When children are more confident, introduce the rhyme. Everyone can repeat it, taking turns to run in and skip.

Elijah, Elijah, what did you do?
I taught Elisha everything I knew.
Elisha, Elisha, what did you do then?
I worked for God with his power again.

When we want to learn a new skill, it is very helpful to have someone else to help us learn – someone who can already do what we are learning to do. Elisha learned all about serving God as a prophet from Elijah.

For younger children:
You could use any simple game that some of the children
know how to play. They can then show the others how to
play. You could still say the rhyme together.

39

Teamwork

2 Chronicles 20:1-13

Key verse: The people of Judah came together to seek help
from the Lord; indeed they came from every
town in Judah to seek him (1 Chronicles 20:4).

Theme: Prayer.

Aim: To emphasize that working together with others
is beneficial. King Jehoshaphat, rather than seek-
ing God alone, brought all his people together to
pray.

Preparation:
You will need a large supply of beanbags or similar.

How to play:
Divide into two or more teams. The aim is to transfer as
many bean bags (or similar small objects) as possible from
one end of the room to another in a given time. Only one
beanbag per person is allowed on each trip.

At the beginning of the game, only one person from each
team is allowed to run back and forth. Once they have delivered three beanbags, they have the option of carrying on
alone, cheered on by their team members, or they can 'free'
one team member on each subsequent trip who can then
start to help.

Position the other team members such that a significant
detour has to be made to 'free' them. It will be sensible to
free team members to help, despite the detour.

This game illustrates that extra effort might be involved to get other people involved, but it's worth it in the long run. When we pray, we can just pray alone, but joining with others can be beneficial too. King Jehoshaphat brought all his people together to pray.

For younger children:
This sort of team game will be too complicated for young children. Try this instead:

Line everyone up at one end of your meeting room. Link arms to form a tight line. Demonstrate how to march in step, starting with the left foot. Left, right, left, right, still keeping the tight line.

Repeat several times, teaching the children this chant:
The more we are together, together, together,
The more we are together, the stronger we will be.

40

Anticipation Frustration

2 Chronicles 36:15-23; Jeremiah 29:10-14

Key verse: This is what the Lord says: 'When seventy years are completed for Babylon, I will come to you and fulfil my gracious promise to bring you back to this place' (Jeremiah 29:10).

Theme: Promises; prayer.

Aim: To emphasize that we often have to wait for God to answer our prayers.

Preparation:

Before the session, freeze a coin inside a block of ice, one for each team of two to four people, using a yoghurt pot or similar as the mould. Make sure that the coin is roughly in the middle. You will also need a stopwatch.

How to play:

Choose one or more of the following activities:

In teams of two to four, challenge the children to reach the coin in the ice without smashing the ice block or using an oven, hot water, etc. The only thing to do is to wait for it to melt. Warming it using their hands will speed up the process slightly, but take care that no one hurts themselves by holding it for too long.

You may need to go on to other activities and come back to this later.

Ask everyone to stand still in a certain position, for example, on one leg or with arms outstretched. Instruct them to try to remain still until you tell them to stop. After one minute, ask them to sit down and let them guess in turn for how long they were standing.

Ask everyone to walk from one side of the room to the other in as close to one minute as possible. They must judge the time and speed for themselves.

Ask everyone to sit with their eyes closed. When they think one and a half minutes has passed they should raise their hand quietly, keeping their eyes shut. Record the number of elapsed seconds when individuals raise their hands. Once everyone's hand is raised, or after about two minutes, stop the activity and tell them the results.

Those activities were all to do with time and waiting.

When you're looking forward to something, anticipating something good, time can seem to pass more slowly. Ask who can remember looking forward to something in the past and allow them to tell everyone about it. Is there anything that they are looking forward to at the moment? The people of Judah were looking forward to something and had been doing so for a long time.

For younger children:
Children under six won't be very good at estimating time. You may prefer to ask them to walk slowly across the room in the time it takes you to count slowly to twenty.

41

Temple-building Relay

Ezra 1:1-11; 3:1-2; 3:7-10; 4:1-4; 6:13-16

Key verse: Anyone of his people among you – may his God be with him, and let him go up to Jerusalem in Judah and build the temple of the Lord, the God of Israel, the God who is in Jerusalem (Ezra 1:3).

Themes: The temple; promises.

Aim: To help the children remember how the temple in Jerusalem was eventually rebuilt after the exile, despite problems, fulfilling God's word.

Preparation:

For each team you will need: Several foil trays and cuddly toys, a good number of boxes and building blocks, cymbals or saucepan lids, a sheet of paper and a pen.

How to play:

Play this relay game in two or more teams. The tasks involved are based on the Jews' journey back to Jerusalem and the building of the temple. When everyone is ready to start, all the teams should count years together in fives 5 years, 10 years, 15 years up to 70 years — representing the seventy years the Jews spent in Babylon.

A number of items representing articles of silver and gold, goods, livestock and gifts (foil trays, cuddly toys, boxes, etc.) must be taken to 'Jerusalem' (i.e. the other end of the room), in relay style.

Everyone must run to 'Jerusalem' together and build the

'altar' (use boxes or wooden blocks).

A 'cymbal' should be crashed five times to represent the completion of the temple foundations (you could use saucepan lids).

A sheet of paper must be taken to a leader for them to sign, representing the time of trouble and the decree needed from King Darius.

The 'temple' should be built using boxes and a loud shout given when it is finished, e.g. 'The temple is finished. Praise the Lord!'

Leaders will need to demonstrate a complete run-through. Teams may need help in remembering what comes next as they progress.

God had promised his people that they would return to Jerusalem and rebuild the city. When Cyrus, king of Persia, came to power, he allowed all Judeans to return to their land and actually commanded that they rebuild the temple. He even sent gifts with them to help, plus all the articles from the temple that had been taken when they had been conquered 70 years before. God fulfilled his promise in a most unexpected way. The builders came up against opposition, but in the end they won through and the temple was finished.

To our eyes, things don't always go smoothly when God fulfils his promises. However, despite the frustrations, God's plans will be completed.

For younger children:
This simple activity makes a similar point and can be used to follow-up the story. When things don't go right for us, or we need to wait patiently, we know we can trust God to work everything out for us in his time.

Stand in a circle and sing the rhyme to the tune, *This old man*. Repeat with actions.

I will trust
God to be *(stamp feet)*
There when things aren't good for me *(spin round on the spot)*
If-I-keep-on-trusting very patiently *(raise joined hands)*
Things will work out best, you'll see! *(one or two children crash cymbals, and everyone says, 'Yeah!')*

Repeat several more times so everyone gets a turn with the cymbals.

42

Pass it on

Ezra 7:1-10, 25-26; Psalm 78:1-8

Key verse: For Ezra had devoted himself to the study and observance of the Law of the Lord, and to teaching its decrees and laws in Israel (Ezra 7:10).

Themes: God's word; discipleship.

Aim: To emphasize how God's word is passed on from generation to generation.

Preparation:

You will need a collection of 10-20 unbreakable objects of various sizes and shapes, the same for each team, e.g. a football, a pencil, a big box, a button. You may like to use items connected with passing on God's word, e.g. a Bible, an audio tape, a video tape, a CD, a song book, an email message, a mobile phone, a microphone.

How to play:

You will need two teams of at least four people – the more in each team, the better.

Line up each team, one behind the other, about one pace apart. At the feet of the first person, place ten to twenty objects or varying size and shape – anything that is not breakable.

The objects must be passed, as quickly as possible, under the legs of the first person and over the next person's head and so on all the way down the line.

First team to pass back all the objects wins.

Ezra had to pass on the Law to a generation of Israelites that knew very little of it due to the exile. They had lived for a long time in a foreign country whose people followed different gods. Every generation needs to pass on God's word to the next so as the children grow up they know God's wise guidelines and the stories of all he has done in the past.

For younger children:
Use objects that are easier to handle – neither very large nor very small. Make one large team to avoid the competitive dimension if you wish. If you use items connected with passing on God's word, you can talk about how they are used.

43

Right, wrong or risk?

Esther 4:1-17; 7:1-10

Key verse: For if you remain silent at this time, relief and deliverance for the Jews will come from another place, but you and your father's family will perish. And who knows but that you have come to royal position for such a time as this (Esther 4:14).

Theme: Faith.

Aim: To emphasize the theme of taking risks for God.

Preparation:

Mark a scale on the floor, from 0 to 100 going up in 10s. Mark one side of the room 'A' and the other 'B'. Make up a series of general knowledge questions with multiple choice answers.

If you have time before the session, watch some of the TV shows that your group enjoy and read some of their magazines. This will give you ideas for questions and help you get to know your young people better. To each question, there must be three possible answers: A, B or C.

A and B will consist of a right and a wrong answer. C will always correspond to 'No Risk', and contestants can choose that if they don't know the answer and don't want to risk a guess.

How to play:

Ask everyone to stand level with the 0 on your scale. If your group is large, choose several volunteers to be the contestants while everyone else can be the audience.

Ask a series of multiple choice questions. Anyone who chooses answer 'A' must turn to face the wall labelled 'A'. Anyone who chooses answer 'B' must turn to face the wall labelled 'B'. Anyone who chooses answer 'C' must sit down.

A right answer wins 10 points and a wrong answer loses 10 points – children should move up or down the scale accordingly (they can stop at 0).

Answering 'C – No Risk' will neither gain nor lose points and children stay in their current position. You could provide a sweet for right answers and a cup of water over the head for wrong answers, if you want to liven things up a bit!

Try to vary the difficulty of the questions so that you can be sure everyone will get some right, but will definitely not know the answers to others, forcing them to guess or opt for C – No Risk.

Throw in a few high risk rounds where a correct answer doubles the contestant's points but a wrong one means they lose them all.

The risks you took in that quiz had no serious consequences – we were just playing a game. In life there are different types of risk:
• **A silly risk involves doing something dangerous for no good reason, e.g. swimming out to sea too far.**
• **A sinful risk involves doing something that is wrong, e.g. skipping a lesson and risking punishment.**
• **A sensible risk involves taking on a challenge, e.g. entering a race where you risk doing badly, but you may do well.**
• **A sensible risk could also be a godly risk – this may involve doing something that God wants you to do, but you know you may risk being called names at school.**

Esther took a godly risk when she wanted to save the lives of her people.

For younger children:
Fix the words where everyone can see them. Help the children to read the rhyme together. Demonstrate the actions with words. Repeat with the children.

God helped Esther find a way	*Everyone kneel.*
To save his people on that day.	*Clasp hands together.*
King Xerxes might be very great,	*Bow down to the ground.*
And Haman, full of powerful hate,	*Shake fist and scowl.*
But God is greater than them all,	*Lift palms to God.*
And answers when his people call.	*Stand with lifted hands.*
Great men or kings, they cannot stand	
	After the words, blow through the mouth.
When God decides to move his hand.	*Raise palms to God.*

44

Gottalots and Havenots

Isaiah 1:10-17

Key verse: Learn to do right! Seek justice, encourage the oppressed. Defend the cause of the fatherless and plead the case of the widow (Isaiah 1:17).

Theme: Sharing.

Aim: To help children to understand injustice.

Preparation:

You will need two tables, some chairs and plenty of breakfast for a small number of children. You will also need a loaf of bread and a jug of water. Check for food allergies.

How to play:

Assign a few children to the 'Gottalots' group. Gottalots should be seated on chairs round a table at one end of the room. Assign most of the group to the 'Havenots' group. 'Havenots' should be seated on the floor at the other end.

Announce that you will now provide breakfast (or lunch/tea) for everyone. Ask them not to start eating immediately. Provide a good meal for the 'Gottalots' (cereals, rolls, croissants, bacon … whatever you can manage) but provide the 'Havenots' (the majority of the group) with just a loaf of bread and jug of water to share between them.

Prior to beginning the meal, explain these rules:

• 'Gottalots' may eat whatever they like but, when they hear a leader ring a bell or blow a whistle they must go to a separate table with a small portion of food (a 'sacrifice') and bow before returning to their breakfast.

- 'Havenots' may only eat the bread and water given to them, but, a few at a time, they may visit the 'Gottalots' and try to obtain extra food by begging or offering to do a task (e.g. pouring the drinks out, serving food, promising to clear up afterwards). The 'Gottalots' can decide whether to share their food. NB You may have to stop this activity if 'Havenots' launch a raid on the 'Gottalots' and things turn nasty! Don't suggest this course of action!

After what you judge to be an appropriate amount of time, stop the activity and discuss the feelings of the 'Havenots' and 'Gottalots'.

It feels very unfair to only be given bread and water while others have lots of delicious food. In fact, there are many places in the world today where people are very poor and have very little to eat. Meanwhile, we often eat too much! Doesn't that seem unfair? In Israel in Bible times many people were very poor while others were very rich. The rich, although they made sacrifices to God and did lots of religious things, treated the poor badly and God was not happy.

Do you think God is happy with us if we sing and pray to him but are not generous to others?

For younger children:
Simply give a few children a selection of cakes, biscuits and fruit and the other children just dry crackers. Allow them to taste the food you have given them and invite them to share. Talk to them about how they feel and what it means for something to be 'not fair'.

45

Clay Pots

Jeremiah 18:1-12; 19:1-3, 10-13

Key verse: Like clay in the hand of the potter, so are you in my hand, O house of Israel (Jeremiah 18:6).

Themes: Obedience; guidance.

Aim: To help the children to understand God's words to Israel, spoken through the prophet Jeremiah, using a clay pot as a visual aid.

Preparation:

You will need play dough for each pair or small group; a plastic covering to protect the table; a selection of cards with names of items that can be made with play dough.

How to play:

Form pairs or small groups. Ask one child from each group to come to you and see what is written on one of the cards. They then go back to their group and make the item from play dough. The others in the group try to guess what they are making. The child doing the modelling must not speak.

First to guess correctly wins a point for their team. The last object to make can be a pot, to introduce the story.

When God wanted to speak to his people about something through the prophets of the Old Testament, he often used a visual aid. In this case, he told Jeremiah to go and watch a potter making clay pots, and then to buy a clay jar to use as he spoke God's word to the elders and priests. God told the people he would treat them

like clay. He could do whatever he liked with them, as the potter moulds the clay. He warned them that he would smash their nation like the clay jar because they had turned away from him.

For younger children:
Form small groups, each with a leader. Choose a child to do the modelling. The leader whispers the name of an object to this child who then makes it. First person to guess what it is becomes the next modeller. For very young children, just have all the children make objects that a leader calls out.

46

Ready, Steady, Cook!

Daniel 1:1-21

Key verse:　　But Daniel resolved not to defile himself with the royal food and wine, and he asked the chief official for permission not to defile himself in this way (Daniel 1:8).

Themes:　　Holiness; miracles.

Aim:　　To help the children remember the story of Daniel and his determination not to disobey God's law in the middle of an idol-worshipping foreign country.

Preparation:

You will need to cut up a large selection of salad vegetables.

How to play:

Pairs of children use salad vegetables (already cut to avoid the need for knives) to try to make an attractive snack or meal. Have a compere and make the activity into a competition like the TV programme *Ready, Steady, Cook!* Set a time limit and invite a chef, cook, or someone else in your church involved in catering to be the judge.

It must have been strange for Daniel and his friends to live in another country. The people in Babylon were very different from Daniel and his friends, and worshipped false gods.

Daniel and his friends asked to be given only vegetables to eat and water to drink, avoiding the food from the king's table. This was because anyone who ate food from the king's table showed themselves to be a supporter of the king. God gave Daniel this good idea to show that they didn't need to eat the king's food to look well. In those days, people were not so concerned with looking lean and fit, but with looking prosperous and wealthy, so to put on weight was considered a good thing.

God made sure that Daniel and his friends looked more well-fed than the others who ate the king's food, which must have been a miracle, if all they had was vegetables and water, while the others ate rich meat and drank wine.

Daniel and his friends worked hard for the king but they were loyal to God first.

For younger children:
Allow everyone to taste a variety of salad vegetables – see who can identify the vegetable they are eating. Or make animals from vegetable pieces and eat them afterwards.

47

All bow down

Daniel 3:1-30

Key verse: They trusted in him and defied the king's command and were willing to give up their lives rather than serve or worship any god except their own God (Daniel 3:28).

Themes: Sin; holiness, worship.

Aim: To emphasize the theme of worshipping only God.

Preparation:

You will need to make a tape or CD with a mixture of short excerpts from Christian and non-Christian songs.

How to play:

This game is similar to musical bumps and musical statues. All the children dance about in the middle of the room while a song is played. When the music stops, they must decide whether to bow down or stand still.

If the song is worship music, they must go down on their knees when it stops. If the song is a pop song they must stand still when it stops. Anyone who does the wrong thing is thrown into the fiery furnace (an area to one side where they must wait) for three turns.

If you want to find a winner, look for children who are quickest at doing the correct action. To make the game a little harder, and to introduce the theme of peer pressure, have a group of children who often choose the wrong action but are immune to being 'out'. This makes the other children have to really think – they can't just watch everyone else! If you have children in the group who will be unfamiliar with praise and worship songs, play excerpts before the game starts so that they know what they are listening for.

Shadrach, Meshach and Abednego were three of Daniel's friends living in Babylon with him. Babylon's king, Nebuchadnezzar, made a huge gold statue and commanded that whenever people heard music play, they must bow down and worship the statue. The three friends refused. They didn't do what everyone else did. They would only worship the one true God.

In the game we just played, we only bowed down when we heard the worship music, music that honours God. We stood still when we heard the other music. The three friends got into huge trouble for refusing to bow down and worship the statue. They were thrown into a fiery furnace. But God rescued them and they came out alive and well.

For younger children:
Use Christian children's songs and nursery rhymes that the children know well.

48

Persuasion

Daniel 6:1-28

Key verse: Then they said to the king, 'Daniel, who is one
of the exiles from Judah, pays no attention to
you, O king, or to the decree you put in writing.
He still prays three times a day' (Daniel 6:13).

Themes: Prayer; temptation.

Aim: To introduce the themes of temptation, persua-
tion and peer pressure.

Preparation:

You will need a small cake and a plate of 'custard pie' foam,
available from party shops.

How to play:

One person is blindfolded, and stood in the middle of the
room. Two others then stand in opposite corners, one with a
cake, one with a handful of shaving foam.

They must try to persuade the blindfolded person to walk
to them and take the 'prize' that they have. Obviously one
'prize' is more desirable than the other, but both 'persuaders'
must try to tempt the blindfolded person to go to them.

Swap roles and let other groups of three take a turn. Who
was the best 'persuader'? Did they lie in order to tempt the
blindfolded volunteer?

**People often try to persuade us to do things. How do we
know whether to listen to them? King Darius was persuaded to make an evil law. Daniel was not persuaded to**

obey it. **King Darius was wrong. Daniel was right. Daniel had committed himself to God as a young man. When he first arrived in Babylon he decided to put God before the king. We must decide to put God first. That will help us know what to do when people try to persuade us.**

For younger children:
Play *Sleeping Lions* as a story reminder. Everyone lies on the floor as sleeping lions. Those who twitch even a whisker are out. The last unmoving lion is the winner.

Explain that Daniel was not saved from death because the lions were asleep. He was saved by God's angel who shut the lions' mouths. He did what was right and God protected him.

49

'nomiS says …'

Jonah 1:1-17

Key verse: But Jonah ran away from the Lord and headed for Tarshish (Jonah 1:3).

Theme: Obedience.

Aim: To help the children remember how Jonah ran away from God and went in the opposite direction.

Preparation:

Write down the list of commands you will use.

How to play:

Play a game using the rules of 'Simon says …' except everyone must do the opposite of what is asked and the leader calls 'nomiS says …' ('Simon' backwards) instead of 'Simon says'.

For example, if the command is to raise the left hand everyone should raise the right. If they are asked to sit down they should stand up. Commands need to be worked out in advance so that there are fairly obvious opposites. Watch out for any of the group who finds 'left and right' activities difficult – they could mark 'L' and 'R' on their hands to help them.

Other examples:
- Turn to your left.
- Stand on your right leg.
- Walk forwards.
- Hop backwards.

• Look upward.
• Put your right hand on your left knee.
• Close your right eye and look down.
• Hold your left ear with your right hand and turn round in a clockwise direction.

You can be 'out' if you fail to do the opposite action or if you move when the caller fails to say 'Nomis says …' prior to the instruction.

Jonah did the opposite of what God asked him. God told Jonah to go to Nineveh but he headed for Tarshish, a town in the opposite direction. But things didn't work out well for Jonah when he disobeyed God.

For younger children:
Play a game of 'Hide and Seek' or simple tag.

50

Second Chances

Jonah 2:1-10; 3:1-10

Key verse:　　Then the word of the Lord came to Jonah a second time: 'Go to the great city of Nineveh and proclaim to it the message I give you' (Jonah 3:1).

Theme:　　Obedience.

Aim:　　To introduce or reinforce the idea that God gives second chances.

Preparation:

Set up the equipment you will require, such as tennis balls and a bucket, a target, some coins, etc.

How to play:

Set up a variety of tasks for everyone to attempt. They should vary in difficulty. Some should be possible to achieve first time. Some should be difficult to achieve first time but possible after several attempts.

　　Example activities:

- Throw a ball into a small container several metres away.
- Aim a paper aeroplane at a target
- Add up a short list of numbers.
- Toss a coin so that it lands on 'heads'.
- Throw a ball up and catch it ten times.
- Balance on one foot for ten seconds.

　　Let everyone have one attempt at each activity. Then let everyone have a second chance to try any activity at which they did not succeed first time. Let them have a third and fourth chance, or more if necessary, to try the more difficult activities. This is not supposed to be a competition so emphasize helping and encouraging each other rather than seeing who is best at certain things. The point is that everyone is able to succeed, so don't make any activity too difficult.

We don't always succeed first time at everything. But we can succeed at many things given more than one attempt. In that game, we were all trying our best from the beginning but most of us needed second chances in order to succeed. Jonah didn't try his best to start with. He disobeyed and did the opposite of what he was asked. But God gave Jonah a second chance to go to Nineveh, even though he disobeyed the first time.

God gives us second chances. Even when God tells us to do something and we fail or disobey, he is willing to forgive us and will often give us a second chance.

For younger children:
Adjust the difficulty of the activities to the age and ability of the children.

51

Into the future

Psalm 130:8; Isaiah 7:14; Isaiah 9:6-7; Isaiah 49:6;
Micah 5:2; Matthew 1:21

Key verse: She will give birth to a son, and you are to give
him the name Jesus, because he will save his peo-
ple from their sins (Matthew 1:21).

Themes: Jesus; Christmas; promises.

Aim: To emphasize that biblical prophecy is accurate.

Preparation:

You will need beanbags and hoops. Mark out a 'timeline' on
the floor using masking tape. Mark off every 100 years from
800BC up 100AD, and tape a piece of card to the floor with
the date at each of these ten points. Place a hoop at around
the date of Jesus birth. Place other hoops just before and
after 700BC.

How to play:

Form teams and assign different coloured beanbags to each
team. Explain what a timeline is and that you are going to
play a game where you throw beanbags along a timeline, aim-
ing at a certain point. Team members take it in turns to throw
beanbags while standing in each of the hoops at 700BC.
Their target is the hoop placed at 0AD. Points are awarded
for every beanbag landing in the hoop.

**Hundreds of years before Jesus' birth, several prophets
spoke about a Saviour who would be born. For example,
both Isaiah and Micah spoke about Jesus around seven**

hundred years before his birth. In the game, you were standing on the timeline at around the 700BC point. You were throwing your beanbags to land 'in the future', near to when Jesus was born. You were doing your best to be accurate. Isaiah and Micah didn't know exactly when Jesus would be born, but God had told them accurate details about the circumstances. (You can then go on to talk about the Old Testament prophecies and the New Testament passages that show their accuracy.)

- Psalm 130:8 (Matthew 1:21)
     God will save his people from their sins.
- Isaiah 7:14 (Matthew 1:22-23)
     Jesus, 'God with us', will be born to a virgin.
- Isaiah 9:6-7 (Luke 1:32-33)
     God's Son will be born.
- Isaiah 49:6 (Luke 2:30-32)
     Jesus will be a 'light for the Gentiles'.
- Micah 5:2 (Matthew 2:6)
     Jesus will be born in Bethlehem.

For younger children:

Hundreds of years have no meaning for small children so don't use the timeline. Instead, have two hoops labelled Isaiah and Micah, placed next to each other. Place a hoop labelled Jesus a short distance away. Children can take it in turns to stand in the 'Isaiah' and 'Micah' hoops and try to throw beanbags into the 'Jesus' hoop. Talk simply about just one of the passages above.

52

Pay attention

Luke 1:5-25, 57-66

Key verse: But the angel said to him: 'Do not be afraid, Zechariah; your prayer has been heard. Your wife Elizabeth will bear you a son, and you are to give him the name John' (Luke 1:13).

Themes: Prayer; Christmas; Jesus.

Aim: To help the children understand that often we are so distracted by the world around us that we don't hear God.

Preparation:

If you play this game in the lead-up to Christmas, you will need a carrier bag for each group plus selection of Christmas items, for example, a Christmas pudding, a piece of tinsel, a wrapped present, a Father Christmas hat. If you play the game at another time of year, a selection of children's games and activities would be appropriate, for example, a video, a CD, a football, a computer game.

How to play:

Divide your group into teams of two to six people and set them off on a continuous relay. Each person must take a carrier bag and then collect the objects placed at intervals in front of them. They then run to touch the far wall, replace the items where they found them and pass the bag to the next team member who repeats the task. Tell the teams that they must keep going, not just run once each. They will be awarded two points for every completed run. Tell them that they will be given a signal to let them know when to stop – for example, they must watch for when you raise one hand in the air. Twenty bonus points will be awarded to the first team to sit down silently behind the start line when you raise your hand.

Allow the relay to continue long enough for everyone to have run at least twice. When you raise your hand, some teams will see immediately while others will be a bit slow on the uptake. The team receiving the bonus points will be the winning team.

In order to win the game you had to look out carefully for the signal to stop. If you became too engrossed in the relay you would miss the signal and miss out on the bonus points.

Some people can miss out on what God is doing or saying because they're too busy to pay attention to him. Most of the religious leaders at the time of Jesus' birth were very busy carrying out their duties religiously but didn't really love God and pay attention to him. They weren't open to what he was doing.

The story of the priest Zechariah shows that he was different.

For younger children:
Play an adapted game of musical statues where the children dance but have to look carefully for when a leader raises their hand at which point they must stand as still as possible. They must not get so engrossed in the dancing that they forget to stop. When most of the children have stopped each time, halt the music and eliminate a few of the children who were slow to stop.

53

Impossible?

Luke 1:26-38

Key verse: For nothing is impossible with God (Luke 1:37).
Themes: Miracles; Christmas; Jesus.
Aim: To introduce the idea of impossibility.

Preparation:
You will need a garden cane or similar, masking tape, two full water carriers and a stopwatch.

How to play:
These three activities can all be made more difficult until they eventually become impossible.

Hold the cane about 1.5m above the ground and ask children to limbo underneath. Once everyone has had a go, lower the cane by about 30cm and repeat. They must stay on their feet and bend their legs, keeping shoulders and head back. If they touch the rod or the floor they are eliminated. Eventually, no one will make it underneath.

Mark a start line with masking tape. Mark another line 50 cm away. Mark four more lines at 50cm intervals, the last being 2.5m from the start line. Ask children to jump, feet together (no run up), from the start line to the first line. Then let them try to jump from the start line to the second line, then the third, and so on. Some will manage the 1m line, some the 1.5m line, and if you have any star athletes, the 2m line. All should find the 2.5m line impossible to reach.

Ask children, in turn, to hold the water carriers out in front of them, keeping arms straight and hands at shoulder level. Ask the first child to hold the position for 5 seconds, the next for 10 seconds, the next for 15 seconds, until the task becomes impossible. (Save some of your older, bigger and stronger children until last for this, but watch out that no-one puts himself under excessive strain.)

Our physical abilities prevent us from doing some things. Some things are impossible because, for example, we are not big enough, small enough, flexible enough or strong enough. Sometimes we think something is impossible but we are proved wrong – it is possible after all.

That's what happens with God's miracles – things we think are impossible, with God, become possible.

No one thought it could be possible that Mary, a virgin, would give birth to God's Son. But as the angel said, '...nothing is impossible with God.'

For younger children:
Omit the limbo-dancing task. Adjust activities 2 and 3 to suit the ability of the children.

54

Who will be with us for Christmas?

Matthew 1:18-25

Key verse: All this will take place to fulfil what the Lord had said through the prophet: 'The virgin will be with child and will give birth to a son, and they will call him Immanuel' – which means, 'God with us' (Matthew 1:22-23).

Themes: Jesus; Christmas; families.

Aim: To help children understand that Jesus is 'Immanuel', God with us. It is designed to be played just before Christmas.

Preparation:

You will need a set of slips of paper for each group on which is written a family name, such as 'Simpson', 'Fowler', 'Patel' or 'Flintstone'. One piece of paper for each group should have written on it 'Great Aunt June' plus the family name. Each group will also need a paper hat, a wrapped present, a balloon, a cracker and a mince pie on a plate.

How to play:

The aim of this game is for each person to find the other members of their 'family' and sit 'Great Aunt June' in a chair with a paper hat, a wrapped present, a balloon, a cracker and a mince pie on a plate.

  Start by giving each person a piece of paper on which is written a family name. If you have a large group, you could have six per family and several families. If your group is small, the game could still work with two families of three.

The first task is for everyone to get into family groups. One of each family will have the name 'Great Aunt June'.

Once in family groups (make sure they know how many of them there should be!), they must sit 'Great Aunt June' in a chair at one end of the room. Then, relay-style, they fetch her various Christmas items from the other end of the room. If you have older children, get them to wrap the present and blow up the balloon to add difficulty.

When she is ready, wearing the hat and holding the present, cracker, balloon and mince pie, the 'family' must shout 'Happy Christmas Great Aunt June!' to finish.

Allow the winning team to eat all the mince pies as a prize. (Check for allergies.)

Ask everyone with whom they will be spending Christmas. **Christmas is traditionally the time when relations and friends come to visit or we go to stay with Grandparents or cousins. But the real meaning of Christmas is not to do with having friends and families with us, fun and important as that may be, but having God with us.**

For younger children:
Choose a helper to be Great Aunt June. Hide Christmas items around the room for the children to search for and bring to her. Have two helpers and two groups looking for different coloured items if you want to make it competitive.

55

Santa's Sack

Luke 2:1-20; Matthew 2:1-12

Key verse: Where is the one who has been born king of the Jews? We saw his star in the east and have come to worship him (Matthew 2:2).

Themes: Christmas; worship.

Aim: To introduce the theme of praise and worship. It is designed to be played at Christmas.

Preparation:

You will need a large number of empty boxes wrapped in Christmas paper (you could play just after Christmas so you've got plenty of paper you can re-use), plus several large sacks/bin liners/pillow cases.

How to play:

The aim of the game is to throw all the 'presents' into a sack, held by a team member. The person holding the sack should stand in a circle or hoop on the floor, with the rest of the team several metres away. It should be difficult, but possible, to get presents into the sack.

On the word 'Go!', team members must step forward to a 'throwing line', pick up a present and aim it at the sack. Then they must go to the back of the team, ready to try again when their turn comes. Each present in the sack is worth ten points and teams have two minutes to get as many presents in a possible. Presents that 'miss' can be retrieved to be thrown again if the supply at the 'throwing line' runs out.

Bonus points can also be awarded. Whenever a team

member succeeds at getting a present into the sack, the rest of the team must cheer madly. A small cheer is worth five extra points, but a really enthusiastic cheer is worth ten points. Assign a leader to each team to keep track of bonus points.

People can really make a noise if they're excited about something. Think about the singing and shouting at football matches or concerts. You all made loads of noise when you were winning points for your teams. This is a type of praise. Praising someone normally involves expressing your admiration or thanks for something they've done. You're saying 'Well done!' When you greatly admire someone, praise is a natural response.

The shepherds and Magi praised and worshipped Jesus at his birth.

For younger children:
Children will need to stand quite close to the sack. Remove the competitive element and use just one sack held by a helper. Choose children to come up one at a time to throw a present. Encourage the rest of the children to clap and cheer even if the present does not go in – they can still praise a good try.

56

Salvation for all

Luke 2:22-38

Key verse: For my eyes have seen your salvation, which you
                  have prepared in the sight of all people, a light
                  for revelation to the Gentiles and for glory to
                  your people Israel (Luke 2:30-32).

Themes: Mission; promises.

Aim: To help the children understand that salvation
                  through Jesus is available to all people, all over
                  the world.

Preparation:

You will need a selection of music from around the world,
plus a large bag containing items of clothing such as a beret;
a Mexican hat; a 'sari' (a long piece of cloth that can be
wrapped around someone will do); a pair of Bermuda shorts;
a kilt; a Chinese coolie's hat. Make sure you have an item for
everyone in the group.

How to play:

Play a game similar to 'Pass the Parcel' but instead of passing a parcel around the group, pass a bag containing various
items of clothing, hats, shoes, etc. that represent different
parts of the world. When the music stops, the person holding the bag must pull out an item of clothing and wear it for
the rest of the session.

Once a person is dressed in something, they should pass
the bag on to the next person if the music stops on them
again – this will ensure everyone gets to wear something.

We can celebrate that Jesus did not come for just one nation or group or type of person, but for everyone. It was predicted before and after his birth that he would bring salvation to people worldwide, and we can celebrate today because now, two thousand years later, in most countries throughout the world, there are Christians.

For younger children:
Play this adapted version of *Musical Chairs* using music from around the world. Each round, place an item of clothing from around the world on one of the chairs. When the music stops, everyone finds a seat. The child with the item of clothing on their chair has a rest for the next round so that a leader can help them to dress up. Keep going until everyone is dressed up.

57

How do you do that?

Luke 2:41-52

Key verse: Jesus grew in wisdom and stature, and in favour
                with God and men (Luke 2:52).

Themes: Jesus; discipleship.

Aim: To introduce the idea that we all need to learn
                new things. It will help children share their own
                experiences of learning and lead into the Bible
                story about Jesus' childhood.

Preparation:

In advance, hide around the room a number of objects connected with learning. For example: Shoe with laces; spelling
list; yo-yo; book; times-tables chart; cup; computer game;
knife and fork; Bible; tie; pen; recorder.

How to play:

Form two teams and give the children a few minutes to find
as many of the hidden objects as possible. You can award
points for every object found. They bring all they find back
to their group area and try to put them in order, starting with
the item they think they learned to use first, e.g. cup.

Award extra points for a well-ordered line of objects.
Then let each child choose an item and bring everyone
together to sit in a big circle. Ask each child the following
questions:

• Have you learned how to use this?
• When did you learn?
• Who taught you?

We've learned to do lots of things but we all have lots more to learn. As Jesus grew up, he had to learn things too, at home and at school. Just like us, he also needed to learn about God.

For younger children:
Have one big team with everyone looking together for the items. Children can bring them straight to the circle and you can talk together in a similar way. Adjust the items used to suit your age group.

58

In the river

Matthew 3:1-17; John 1:19-34

Key verse: Then Jesus came from Galilee to the Jordan to be baptized by John (Matthew 3:13).

Themes: Obedience; Jesus.

Aim: To help the children remember that Jesus was baptised in the river Jordan.

Preparation:
Make a line on the floor with chalk or tape.

How to play:
Children line up next to each other on the line. One side of the line is the river. The other side is the riverbank. A helper can call out a rapid stream of instructions, 'In the river,' 'On the bank,' and children must jump as directed. The speed will ensure that some children will make a mistake and need to sit down, temporarily out of the game. Begin with a trial run so that everyone understands how to play.

Add in a couple of extra instructions to make it harder, e.g. 'Under the waterfall' (hands over head); 'Over the weir' (swimming action).

John baptized people in the River Jordan. Jesus asked John to baptize him, too. Jesus loved God and wanted to obey him. Jesus showed he was ready to start God's work.

For younger children:
Slow down the instructions. Children don't need to be 'out'.

59

Temptometer

Luke 4:1-13

Key verses: Jesus, full of the Holy Spirit, returned from the Jordan and was led by the Spirit in the desert, where for forty days he was tempted by the devil (Luke 4:1-2).

Themes: Temptation; sin.

Aim: To introduce the topic of temptation.

Preparation:
Prepare a list of possible temptations relevant to the children in your group, such as that below. Tape or draw a giant 'temptometer' on the floor with temperatures from 0 to 100 degrees centigrade, going up in tens.

How to play:
Stand the children in a line a couple of metres from the 'temptometer' so that they can see it. Call out temptations such as those below. Children decide how tempted they would feel in each situation.

1 Copying someone else's answers during a test.
2 Moving one of your friend's pawns in a chess game while they are answering the phone.
3 Taking a pound coin that you find on the classroom floor.
4 Watching an '18' video at a friend's house.
5 Losing your temper when asked to tidy your room yet again.
6 Eating the last donut when you know it was saved for your brother.

7 Not giving any money away so you can save for a bike.
8 Swearing when you're stuck on your homework.
9 Lying to try and get a friend out of trouble.
10 Hiding your sister's worst CD so that she can't play it.

After each temptation is read out, children choose a temperature to stand beside. If they would be very tempted by what you have read out, they stand near to 90 or 100 degrees; if not at all tempted, near to 0 degrees; if a little tempted, near to 20 or 30 degrees, and so on.

Explain that it does not matter what other people choose, they must make up their own mind. There are not right and wrong answers.

Some temptations are harder to resist than others. Different people find different things more tempting.

If you resist a temptation again and again, you will probably find it becomes easier to resist. If you give in to temptation, you will probably give in more and more. Feeling tempted is not sin, but giving in is.

Jesus was tempted but he did not give in. He used words from the Bible to help him fight.

For younger children:
Make two teams each with a helper, separated by a row of chairs. Mark a line one metre from the chairs on both sides. Give each team equal amounts of newspaper. Allow a few minutes for teams to tear and make paper ball ammunition.

Set a time limit, and on a given signal both teams must throw paper balls over the chairs and lines into enemy territory.

Team members can fend off opposing missiles, knocking them into the space between the line and the chairs. Missiles received may be thrown back into the opposing camp. When time is up, the team with the least number of opposition missiles behind their line is the winner. Some of the children might be tempted to cheat at the end, moving missiles after the time is up.

Afterwards, explain what temptation is (i.e. wanting to do something you know is wrong, such as cheating in a game). Say that you're going to learn about fighting temptation. They have just been fighting using newspaper. We can fight temptation using words from the Bible, like Jesus did.

60

Follow me!

Matthew 4:18-22

Key verse: 'Come, follow me,' Jesus said, 'and I will make you fishers of men' (Matthew 4:19).

Themes: Discipleship; Jesus.

Aim: To introduce the theme of following Jesus.

How to play:

Sit everyone in a circle. Choose a player to begin.

This player performs one simple action such as clapping hands, twiddling thumbs, scratching head. The next player on the left must perform this action and add another, different one. Play continues around the circle with everyone performing previous actions and adding another.

Continue playing until someone forgets or makes a mistake. That player begins a new sequence of actions.

We all tried to follow the actions exactly in that game. Jesus wants us to follow him and copy his actions. What did Jesus do? Children respond.

Jesus spent time talking and listening to God. So should we. Jesus was kind to people who no one else wanted to be with. So should we be.

Jesus always spoke the truth. So should we. Jesus was obedient to God his Father. So should we be.

For younger children:

Make up a simple obstacle course and ask children to follow a leader to complete it.

61

Chain He

John 1:35-45

Key verse: The first thing Andrew did was to find his brother Simon and tell him, 'We have found the
Messiah' (that is, the Christ) (John 1:41).

Themes: Discipleship; Jesus.

Aim: To help the children understand that Jesus wants
his disciples to tell others about him.

How to play:

One person is 'it' and the others have to try to keep away.
When 'it' manages to touch someone, the two link arms and
work as a pair to get another.

The third joins them and forms quite a formidable part-
nership in their quest for a fourth, etc. Eventually, all but one
are in the chain and can easily surround the last player.

Play this several times.

**The first player each time was trying to get more and
more players to join him. Jesus wants more and more
people to join him. Why was it easier to get others to
join you when you had several people in the chain
already? How is that like talking to people about Jesus?**

(We are not alone, and it's easier when there are others to help.)

For younger children:

Gradually form a long 'snake' with children holding waists
one behind the other. To determine who joins the 'snake'
next, call out categories such as 'anyone wearing red', 'anyone

with a big brother', etc. The child at the head of the line can choose the route around the room and whether they walk, jog, hop, etc.

62

Robbers

Matthew 9:9-13

Key verse: On hearing this, Jesus said, 'It is not the healthy
                who need a doctor, but the sick' (Matthew 9:12).
Theme: Sin.
Aim: To introduce the topic of greed as sin, relating to
                Jesus calling Matthew.

Preparation:
You will need four hoops, one in each of the four corners of
the room. In the middle of the room, place seven beanbags
or other appropriate small objects.

How to play:
Ideally for this game you will need four teams of two or
more people, but you could adapt it for smaller numbers. Try
to find a space outside if your room is small.

Teams are positioned in the four corners of your playing
area, each with a hoop or container. In the middle of the area
place seven beanbags or other small objects. When given the
signal to start, one player from each team must run to the
middle, grab a beanbag and take it back to her team. The next
team member then runs and collects another beanbag. The
aim is to get four beanbags into their team's hoop.

Clearly, after a couple of trips to the middle there will be
no more beanbags left there. At this point they may start to
run to other teams' hoops and steal their bean bags, one at a
time. While they are doing this, of course, they may have
their own beanbags stolen. Mention this aspect of the game

before you start, as some children may simply give up when there are no more bags to take from the middle.

As soon as one team has four bean bags in their hoop, they have won that round. No throwing of beanbags is allowed and only one beanbag per player per trip is permitted. Depending on the numbers in each team and their fitness level, more rounds can be played.

It was fun to try and steal beanbags from other teams, but not so much fun when someone stole from your team. In real life, taking things from other people without their permission will obviously get you into trouble. Stealing and being greedy are sinful.

When Jesus met Matthew, who was to become one of his disciples, Matthew was a tax collector. Tax collectors tended to be selfish, greedy, always taking other people's money and labelled 'sinners' by the Pharisees. (See below which will help children understand what a tax collector is.)

For younger children:
Hide a mixture of real coins, chocolate coins and plastic coins around the room. Children collect as many as they can find. At the end, come together and say that you will now pretend to be a tax collector.

Tell the children they must all give you one of their coins and that, in Bible times, this would have paid for things like for the road to be repaired and the salaries of soldiers and Roman officials. Now ask for two more coins from each child. Explain that tax collectors often took extra money for themselves. This was wrong.

Matthew was a tax collector. Share out and eat the chocolate coins afterwards.

63

Friends like these

Matthew 22:37-39; Mark 12:28-34

Key verses: Jesus replied: 'Love the Lord your God with all your heart and with all your soul and with all your mind.' This is the first and greatest commandment. And the second is like it: 'Love your neighbour as yourself' (Matthew 22:37-39).

Themes: Love; obedience.

Aim: To help the children understand how other people like to be treated.

Preparation:

Prepare a list of ways that someone might show love to someone else. Examples are given below. You will also need two cardboard hearts, some blu-tack and two pieces of card on which are written the numbers 1, 2 and 3.

How to play:

Children should form pairs. Ask them to choose people they think they know the best. You could invite family members in to take part in this game to pair up with their child/brother/sister.

Each pair takes part one at time with others watching. Stand partners facing each other, several metres apart with a music stand or similar in front of them. Each of them will need a heart with blu-tack on the back and a piece of card.

A leader then reads out three possible ways that someone could show love to someone else.

Example:

1 Someone gives you some new clothes.
2 Someone takes you to McDonalds's for lunch.
3 Someone gives you £5.

One of each pair must decide which they would most appreciate and sticks their heart to the appropriate number on their card.

Their partner must guess which they think the first person has chosen and sticks their heart to the appropriate number on their card. Both then show their cards and reveal whether they have managed to pick the same answer. If so, they can swap roles.

If the other partner also manages to guess correctly, they deserve a small prize each, e.g. a heart-shaped sweet. Then bring on the next pair.

Other examples:

1 Someone helps you when you're in trouble.
2 Someone takes you to a theme park for a day.
3 Someone gives you a hug.

1 Someone buys you tickets to see a Premiership football match.
2 Someone gives you a £20 music voucher.
3 Someone often says 'well done' to you and encourages you.

1 Someone helps with your homework.
2 Someone buys you tickets to see a famous musical.
3 Someone offers to cook you your favourite meals for a week.

When we know someone well, it is easier to imagine what they would like. What someone else would like is

not always the same as what we would like, but if we think about the way we like to be treated and the things we like to be given, that will help us to treat other people in a loving and caring way. Think about what people like when you put into practice Jesus' command to 'love your neighbour as yourself'.

For younger children:

Cut out paper hearts and write an answer such as one of those below on each heart. Give out the paper hearts. After each question, help children discover who has the right answer. Repeat the question and the child can read their answer aloud. They can stick their heart to a poster on the wall.

Example:

• Tell me how you like to be treated when you're upset or hurt. *(Looked after and loved.)*

• Tell me how you like to be treated when you've told lies or been unkind, and are sorry. *(Forgiven and loved.)*

• Tell me how you like to be treated when you're in trouble and need someone to talk to. *(Someone to listen to me.)*

64

The Wedding Photo

John 2:1-11

Key verse: This, the first of his miraculous signs, Jesus performed in Cana of Galilee. He thus revealed his glory and his disciples put their faith in him (John 2:11).

Themes: Miracles; Jesus; families.

Aim: To help the children remember the story of Jesus at the wedding in Cana.

Preparation:

You will need to collect various 'wedding' props such as 'veils', rings, bow ties, flowers, etc.

How to play:

In advance, prepare several sets of four slips of paper, enough for everyone in the group, on which are written the words 'Bride', 'Groom', 'Best Man' and 'Bridesmaid'. Each set should also be labelled with a local town or village name. Give each person a folded slip of paper.

On the word 'Go' they look at the slip which tells them their identity for the game and the town/village of their wedding celebration. 'Brides' then have to fetch a 'veil' (e.g. piece of net curtain), 'Grooms' fetch a bow tie, 'Best men' fetch a 'ring', and 'Bridesmaids' fetch a flower, all of which have been distributed in different corners of the room. They then have to find the other three people with the same town/village name and stand posed for a photo, shouting 'Cheese' together when ready.

Jesus and his disciples were invited to a wedding. It was here that he performed his first miracle, or 'sign', as he changed water into wine.

Changing water into wine does not seem as big a miracle as others Jesus performed.

However, for the disciples it was very important. The purpose of this miracle was more significant than simply saving embarrassment for the host and meeting the need of the guests. This first miracle began to reveal Jesus' identity – he showed the power of the God over nature and the love of God who cares for individuals.

Alternative, or in addition:
Provide small amounts of several different varieties of cola in plastic cups and ask group members to identify which is 'Value'/low sugar/caffeine-free/real Coca-Cola etc. Which would they bring out first at a party? (This relates to verse 10.)

For younger children:
Hold a dressing-up race where girls dress up as a 'bride' with veil (use a net curtain), dress (use a nightie), flowers and necklace, and boys dress up as a 'groom' with jacket, waistcoat, hat and bow tie.

65

Mat Race

John 5:1-15; Mark 2:1-12; Matthew 9:1-8; Luke 5:17-26

Key verse: Then Jesus said to him, 'Get up! Pick up your mat and walk.'

Themes: Miracles; Jesus.

Aim: To introduce, or help the children remember any of the stories where Jesus heals someone who cannot walk.

Preparation:

You will need a mat or old sheet/curtain for each team. (Think carefully about how you will deal with this topic if you have children in your group with physical disabilities.)

How to play:

For this activity you will need at least two teams of at least three people. You will also need some space, either inside or outside. The object is for one person to be dragged on some sort of mat (an old curtain or sheet would do) by the rest of the team from one end of the area to the other as quickly as possible.

When they reach the other end, the person who has been carried must jump off and run back to the start carrying their 'mat'. To lengthen the race, give each person a turn at being carried, but be sensitive to the varying ages/sizes of young person in each team.

Those races were fun but it must be very frustrating to never be able to use your legs properly. Think about all

the things that you wouldn't be able to do if you couldn't walk. The Bible tells us several stories about how Jesus healed people who could not walk.

For younger children:
Have a go at any sort of race where use of the legs is limited, e.g. hopping, wheelbarrow, piggyback.

66

Guess the Object

Mark 8:22-26; Mark 10:46-52; John 9:1-6

Key verse: Then his eyes were opened, his sight was
                 restored, and he saw everything clearly (Mark
                 8:25).

Themes: Miracles; Jesus.

Aim: To help the children remember the two-stage
                 healing of the blind man, and to think about
                 what it must be like for people who cannot see
                 properly.

Preparation:

You will need a sheet or screen, a bright lamp and a variety
of objects. (Think carefully about how to deal with this topic
if you have visually impaired children in your group.)

How to play:

Set up a sheet and bright lamp so that shadows can be seen
on the other side of the sheet when objects are placed
between the lamp and the sheet. Form two or more teams.
One team should hold up objects one at a time behind the
sheet screen. The other team tries to guess what the objects
are from the shadows they can see.

The position in which the objects are placed will obviously dramatically effect the shadow formed. For example, a
teapot could be very easy to identify or very difficult depending on which way round it is placed. Allow the guessing team
two chances to guess.

If they can guess the shadow the first time, when the

object's shadow is very difficult to guess, award five points. If they guess the object once it is turned round to make the shadow clearer, award two points. After five to ten objects, the teams swap roles. They could also guess team members' identities.

Jesus' miracle of healing was great for the blind man and his friends who brought him. What a fantastic and life-changing thing to happen! I wonder whether the disciples thought back to Jesus' words earlier when he'd asked them if they still did not see?

In Mark's gospel, we can see the connection between the two occasions. Many people don't understand who Jesus is or what his teaching means. They are like the blind man who could not see a thing. Other people have varying degrees of understanding, but things aren't totally clear. They can be compared to the blind man when he saw the vague outline of people walking.

In the end the blind man could see clearly – Christians will only understand and see totally clearly in heaven (1 Corinthians 13:9-12).

For younger children:
Place a variety of objects under a cloth on a tray. Individuals, one at a time, should feel an object through the cloth and try to guess what it is. If they don't guess correctly, they can then feel the object with their hands under the cloth and guess again. This should make it easier to tell what it is.

Finally, they can remove the object to check whether they are right.

67

Alive not dead

John 11:1-44

Key verse: Jesus said to her, 'I am the resurrection and the
               life. He who believes in me will live, even though
               he dies ...' (John 11:25).

Themes: Miracles; Jesus.

Aim: To help the children remember the story of the
               raising of Lazarus.

Preparation:

You will need several toilet rolls – not too cheap as inexpen-
sive ones can have a tendency to break more easily!

How to play:

Make teams, each selecting a Lazarus. Team members wrap
Lazarus with the paper, trying not to break the roll and using
it completely.

When everyone has finished, on 1-2-3 Go! the first
Lazarus to get out of his bandages will win for his team.
Team members can cheer and encourage their Lazarus, but
not help him.

**Jesus raised Lazarus from the dead to show that he had
power over death. People could see even more clearly
that he was God's Son. To Jesus, death is no stronger
than sleep.**

**The New Testament writers tend to speak of sleep
rather than death (Acts 7:60; 1 Thessalonians 4:13-15
and 5:10).**

When Jesus raised Jairus' daughter (Luke 8:41-42, 49-56), he wakes her from death with the words her mother would have used to wake her up in the morning.

For younger children:
Play a game of *Sleeping Lions*. The children lie very still for as long as possible. The last person to move is the winner.

68

Trust Games

Matthew 14:22-33; Mark 6:45-51; John 6:16-21

Key verse: Immediately Jesus reached out his hand and
                 caught him. 'You of little faith,' he said, 'why did
                 you doubt?' (Matthew 14:31)

Themes: Jesus; miracles; faith.

Aim: To help the children to understand the concept
                 of trust.

How to play:

Have groups of four to six similarly sized children stand
shoulder to shoulder in a circle facing outward and keeping
their bodies rigid.

It should be possible for everyone to lean back against
each other, each supported by the others, like the poles of a
tepee. It may be easier if they start close together and gradually walk their feet outwards.

Next, form the circle again, this time with everyone facing clockwise. It should be possible for everyone to sit down
on the knees of the person behind them.

Both these activities may take some practice!

**These activities both need everyone to trust everyone
else. If anyone has doubts and does not put their trust
in everyone else, the circle will collapse. Peter had to
trust Jesus in order to walk on the water. As soon as he
doubted, he began to sink. We need to trust Jesus and
focus on him, especially when circumstances are difficult and we might easily be distracted.**

For younger children:
Leaders can lead a short chain of blindfolded children through a simple obstacle course. They need to trust the leader in order to complete it successfully.

69

Bread

Matthew 14:13-21; Mark 6:32-44; Luke 9:10-17;
John 6:1-13, 35

Key verse: Jesus then took the loaves, gave thanks, and dis-
                 tributed to those who were seated as much as
                 they wanted. He did the same with the fish (John
                 6:11).

Themes: Miracles; Jesus; sharing.

Aim: To help the children remember the story of
                 Jesus feeding the 5000 and to learn about Jesus'
                 identity as 'the bread of life'.

Preparation:

Collect together a sample of the following types of bread.
All of these should be available at supermarkets:

Wholemeal; granary; fruit; pitta; naan; tortilla; brioche;
rye; unleavened; bagel; muffin. Remove the packaging and
display the bread around the room on separate plates numbered 1 - 11.

Draw out a numbered blank grid to fit the answers shown
opposite and copy it so that you have one for each pair in
your group. Write a few letters in to help the children get
started. Once completed, the grid will read 'Bread of life'
down the middle.

How to play:

Display the breads without packaging and ask everyone,
working in pairs, to go round the room trying to identify each
one, filling in the grid as they go. Tell them that when the grid

is correctly completed, down the middle will be found a description Jesus gave himself. The winning pair will be the first with the grid correctly completed.

1						**B**	a	g	e	l
2			g	r	a	n	a	**R**	y	
3			b	r	i	o	c	h	**E**	
4						n	a	**A**	n	
5	u	n	l	e	a	v	e	n	e	**D**
6							t	**O**	r	t	i	l	l	a
7					m	u	f	**F**	i	n	
8					w	h	o	**L**	e	m	e	a	l
9						p	**I**	t	t	a	
10							**F**	r	u	i	t
11						r	y	**E**			

Today we're going to look at a miracle that involved the production of a large quantity of bread.

The miracle is a sign pointing to Jesus' identity in a similar way to the wine miracle that John wrote about earlier in his gospel – Jesus demonstrated his power over the created world and the love of God for people in need.

Later, Jesus spoke further about this miracle and told the people, 'I am the bread of life' (John 6:25-59).

With older groups, discuss briefly: Why did Jesus call himself the bread of life? (*E.g. Bread was the primary source of nourishment for his audience, and it still is today for millions of people all over the world. He wanted to show that he could satisfy the hunger in the human heart. Bread is a basic food universally — he fulfils this need for everyone. People experiment with every form of material, physical and spiritual solution to fill the inner emptiness of the heart but only Jesus can fully satisfy.)*

For younger children:

After telling the story, emphasize the fact that the boy gave the little bit of food he had and Jesus used it in a big way. We have things that may seem small to us but Jesus can use them in a big way too.

Ask children to draw or write on small 'Post-It' notes some gifts they might give to God. Examples: Time, prayer, worship, kindness to a friend. Make two teams and when each team has ten or twelve gifts written out, form two queues.

On the word of command, they can relay race the other team to stick gifts one at a time onto A4 sized sheets of wrapping paper blu-tacked to the wall.

70

John 3:16 Pentathlon

John 3:1-18

Key verse: For God so loved the world that he gave his one
and only Son that whoever believes in him shall
not perish but have eternal life (John 3:16).

Themes: Salvation; Jesus; forgiveness; sin; love.

Aim: To help children to remember each part of the
key message that Jesus gave Nicodemus.

Preparation:

Set up five stations around the room (you may do better outside if that is possible).

- Station 1: Using cones, cups or other markers mark a
  heart shape on the floor. Leave gaps between the markers.
  You will also need a hockey stick or similar and a small
  ball.
- Station 2: You will need a large ball, or, ideally, an inflat-
  able or stuffed globe.
- Station 3: You will need one hoop and one beanbag.
- Station 4: You will need five plastic cups balanced on the
  edge of a table or a plank, plus five beanbags or small
  balls.
- Station 5: No equipment necessary, although a gym mat
  would be helpful.

How to play:

Here are the instructions for each station. There are passwords
that must be said after each activity before they can go on to
the next one.

- Station 1: Dribble the ball in and out of the markers so that you go all the way round the heart shape. Passwords: God so loved
- Station 2: Bounce the ball against the wall (older children) or on the floor (younger children) ten times. (If the ball doesn't bounce well, children can throw and catch with a leader instead.) Passwords: the world
- Station 3: You have one attempt to throw the one bean-bag into the one hoop positioned a few metres away. (Five second penalty if they miss.) Passwords: that he gave his one and only Son
- Station 4: Knock the five cups off by throwing the bean-bags/balls. (Five second penalty for each cup still standing.) Passwords: that whoever believes in him shall not perish
- Station 5: Lie on the floor then jump up in the air. Repeat five times. Passwords: but have eternal life

Time each child as they complete all five activities.

Jesus' message to Nicodemus has become one of the most famous parts of the whole Bible. John 3:16 sums up why Jesus came. God loves the people of the world, even though they are so sinful. He loves all of us so much that he sent Jesus to die for our sins. He wants everyone to believe in Jesus so that we are saved from the result of our sin. He wants to give us all eternal life.

For younger children:
Activities can be adapted as necessary for younger children. Most will need a leader to tell them the passwords each time so that they can repeat them. Omit the competitive element.

71

Zac's turn-around relay

Luke 19:1-9

Key verse: But Zacchaeus stood up and said to the Lord, 'Look, Lord! Here and now I give half my possessions to the poor, and if I have cheated anybody out of anything, I will pay back four times the amount' (Luke 19:8).

Themes: Sin; Jesus; forgiveness; salvation.

Aim: To help the children to remember the story of Zacchaeus and how he changed after meeting Jesus.

Preparation:

You will need several chairs or a bench at one end of the room. You will need to make a large number of big 'silver coins', or use beanbags to represent moneybags.

How to play:

Form several teams and line them up at one end of the room. Halfway down the room place one 'coin' per team. At the other end of the room place a chair for each team or a bench (the teams can share a bench). Underneath the chairs place piles of 'coins', enough for each team member to collect three.

Each team member must run, pick up the 'coin', step onto the chair, turn round whilst standing on it (leaders may need to hold chairs firm), step down, pick up three more coins, place all four coins where they found the first one, and run back to their team. Then the next person can run, collecting one coin from the first pile and adding three more. Repeat the process until everyone has had a turn.

The idea is that each person is playing the part of Zacchaeus. Before he met Jesus, he took money from people unlawfully (represented by the first coin). He met Jesus after climbing a tree to see him.

After meeting Jesus his life was turned around (represented by turning round on the chair/bench). For everything he had stolen, he gave back four times the amount (represented by taking back the four coins).

Meeting Jesus totally changed Zacchaeus' life. He used to cheat and steal but he realised that to follow Jesus meant turning his back on his old way of life. He decided to give generously to the poor and to compensate the victims of his dishonesty.

When we decide to follow Jesus we all have things we need to turn our back on. It might not be to do with stealing and being greedy, but there are other ways we have all been selfish and sinful.

For younger children:
Give each child a 'coin' with a different number or colour on it. Place three coins for each child around the room with numbers/colours that match the children's first coins. Each child must find three coins that match the one they have been given, e.g. all the number 2 coins.

72

Find the lost sheep

Luke 15:1-7

Key verse: Suppose one of you has a hundred sheep and loses one of them. Does he not leave the ninety-nine in the open country and go after the lost sheep until he finds it? (Luke 15:4)

Themes: Salvation; love; parables; Jesus.

Aim: To help the children to remember the story and message of the Parable of the Lost Sheep.

Preparation:

Cut one hundred pieces of wool of approximately equal length (about 10cm) and place them all around the room. If possible use other rooms too. Ninety-nine of the pieces of wool should be fairly easy to find, but place one piece in a completely hidden and very unlikely location, e.g. the bottom of a mug full of drink.

How to play:

Challenge your group to collect all one hundred pieces of wool – you may need to give some clues to help them to find the last one.

If the weather is fine and you a have safe area that would be suitable, do this activity outside. If you have a large group, plenty of space and someone to help you place the wool pieces, cut two hundred pieces: one hundred of one colour and one hundred of another colour. You can then split the group into two teams for the search. Only give a prize if all one hundred wool pieces are found.

(Obviously, you could use a similar activity using coins for the Parable of the Lost Coin.)

What have you lost recently? How long did it take to find it? How long would you spend looking for each of the following lost items before giving up – a fifty pence piece; a twenty pound note; a favourite earring; your school PE shirt; a pet cat; your front door key; a signed photo of a celebrity; your little brother or sister lost on the beach?

Sheep were very valuable to people in Bible times. Jesus used this story to help people to understand how valuable they are to God.

For younger children:
Use fewer pieces of wool and make them easier to find. Alternatively, children can take it in turns to hide and look for a small toy sheep.

73

Big Spender

Luke 15:11-32

Key verse: But we had to celebrate and be glad, because this brother of yours was dead and is alive again; he was lost and is found (Luke 15:32).

Themes: Forgiveness; sin; love; Jesus; salvation; families; parables.

Aim: To introduce the story of the Lost Son and learn about God's forgiveness.

Preparation:

Using sheets of A4 paper or card numbered 1-30, lay out a 'life size' board game pathway around your room. On certain numbers, add instructions such as the following:

- Spend £200 on designer clothes.
- Spend £100 on CDs.
- Lose £100 on arcade games.
- Spend £100 on playstation games.
- Spend £400 on a new bike.
- Spend £50 on trainers.
- Pay a £500 hotel bill.
- Spend £150 at a restaurant
- Pay a £150 mobile phone bill.
- Spend £250 on train fares.
- Move forward two steps.

Bring in 'props' if possible to make the game more visual.

Make sure that instructions occur every two or three steps

so that there is a high likelihood of players landing on 'spend' numbers. On numbers 28, 29 and 30 write 'Blow any money left on a party and move on to the finish'.

How to play:

To start the game, give each player '£1000' in '£50 notes' (use monopoly money or make paper money) and let them take turns to roll a die. Players physically move forward according to the number on the die and follow any instruction written on the number on which they land. Money 'spent' should be handed to a leader. Any player spending all their money before they reach the end can use up one go taking out a 'loan' from the 'bank' (the leader with the money). It will be fairly difficult for players to reach the end without losing all their money.

The first person to reach the end, having spent all their money, is the 'winner'. The prize however should be something revolting and undesirable – e.g. an ice cream tub full of 'pig swill' made from left over food and vegetable peelings mixed with water. (Don't let them eat this!) You could give every player a prize when they finish – those with no money receive 'pig swill' while those with money left can exchange each '£50 note' for a biscuit or sweet.

That activity gave examples of some of the ways a young person nowadays might choose to spend their money. It can be very easy to spend a lot of money in order to have a good time, but, of course, if you spend too much money all at once it soon runs out.

If you live with your family, if your money runs out you might not have much fun but at least you still have somewhere to live and food to eat.

Today's story is about a young guy who demanded a

huge amount of money from his father, left home, spent it all and then ended up in trouble.

For younger children:
Place two sets of these seven objects in two sacks: a purse; a food take-away leaflet; a toy pig; a map; a card with the word 'sorry' written on it; a pair of sandals; a pack of small cakes.

After the story, form two teams. Children from both teams take it in turns to pick out an object from their team sack. With the help of a leader, the teams try to put the objects in order so that they are reminded of the story. Once finished, they can share the cakes.

Talk to them about how happy God is when someone is sorry and turns back to him.

74

Hard, Shallow, Thorny, Good

Matthew 13:1-23; Mark 4:1-20; Luke 8:4-15

Key verse: But the seed on good soil stands for those with a noble and good heart, who hear the word, retain it, and by persevering produce a crop (Luke 8:15).

Themes: God's word; parables; Jesus.

Aim: To help the children remember and understand the parable of the sower.

Preparation:

Divide your playing area into four by drawing a big cross, or using masking tape.

How to play:

Explain to the children that each area represents a different type of soil: hard; shallow; thorny; good. Show them an action that fits with each type of soil and let them practise each one.

On the hard ground they should curl up in a ball like a little seed that is not growing.

On the shallow ground they should kneel up and then flop on to one side, like a seed that has started to grow but wilted.

On the thorny ground they should kneel up and place their own hands loosely around their neck as though something is choking them. This is to represent a seed that has tried to grow but has been choked by thorny plants around it.

On the good ground they should stand up straight, hands in the air, like a seed that is growing well.

To start the game, stand all the children near the middle of the cross. Shout out different types of soil in turn. The children run to the right area and show the correct action. Have a few practice runs.

To make it competitive, allow the quickest children to the correct area with the correct action to stay 'in'. Pick out a few who are in the wrong area, doing the wrong action, or last to get there, to be 'out'. After a few rounds you will have your winner(s).

Jesus told the story of the soil and the seeds to help us understand what happens when we hear the word of God.

We might be like hard ground – if we don't take any notice of God's word we are like hard ground where nothing can grow. We might be like shallow ground – if we listen a little bit but don't do what God says we are like shallow ground where seeds grow a little and then wither and die.

We might be like thorny ground – if we listen and try to do what God wants and then get distracted by other things we are like thorny ground where seeds try to grow but get choked by other plants. We should try to be like good soil – if we listen well and try to do what God wants we are like good soil where seeds grow well.

For younger children:
The children will need help to remember which area is which. Have several helpers participating with them. You may decide you don't need the competitive element for the children to have fun.

75

Fastest Samaritan

Luke 10:25-37

Key verse: But a Samaritan, as he travelled, came where the man was; and when he saw him, he took pity on him (Luke 10:33).

Themes: Love; Jesus; parables.

Aim: To help the children remember the story of the Good Samaritan and Jesus' teaching about our 'neighbours'.

Preparation:

You will need a piece of cloth that can be used as a sling and two bandages for each group of three. If you know a First Aider or someone else who can bandage efficiently, invite them along to help.

How to play:

Form groups of three. One person in each triplet plays the part of the victim whilst the others play the parts of the Good Samaritan and his donkey.

Before you start, if possible, have someone demonstrate how to put on a sling, bandage a foot and bandage someone's head. Give the groups three minutes to bandage up their victim and carefully carry him or her to the other end of the room.

If you like, donkeys can help with the bandaging, and Samaritans can help with the carrying. Award marks for good bandaging and careful carrying.

The Samaritan in Jesus' story bandaged up the man who had been attacked and took him to an inn to be cared for. Jesus told this story after a man asked him, 'Who is my neighbour?' Jesus wanted to show that it is not just people we know and like to whom we should show love.

Samaritans were hated by Jews so they would have found Jesus' story very surprising. Why would a Samaritan help a Jew? Jesus wanted to show that loving your neighbour as yourself means going out of your way to help all types of people, not just people like yourself.

For younger children:
Bandage dolls or, if you think bandaging is a bit beyond the children in your group, play a game about differences. Children can run to different sides of the room depending on whether, for example, they like or don't like carrots, they have or don't have a dog, they are boys or girls, etc. Some people decide they don't like others just because they are different. Explain that Jesus wants us to care for others even if they are not our friends or different in some way.

76

Scrap heap challenge

Matthew 25:14-30; Luke 19:11-27

Key verse: To one he gave five talents of money, to another two talents, and to another one talent, each according to his ability. Then he went on his journey (Matthew 25:15).

Themes: Jesus; parables; talents.

Aim: To help the children to remember that they should use what they have to the best of their ability.

Preparation:

You will need a large selection of clean scrap materials, e.g. boxes, bottle tops, paper, yoghurt pots, fabric.

How to play:

Form teams of three or four. Give each team an area covered with newspaper and a supply of scrap materials, scissors, string, glue and sticky tape. Give the teams ten minutes to make a model using as many of the materials as possible.

There is no limit to what they can make – it is totally up to them and their imagination. Examples: vehicles, space stations, theme park rides, buildings, robots. The key thing is that they try to use everything they have been given.

When the time is up, judge the models awarding points according to good use of materials design and attractiveness.

Jesus' story of the Talents is about making the most of what you have been given. You were using scrap

materials to make the best model you could. **Perhaps you could have made something better with different materials, but the point is that you did your best with what you had.**

Two of the men in Jesus' story used their money well but one man just hid it and did nothing with it. The first two men were rewarded but the third man was punished. God gives us all sorts of things – money, possessions, talents and abilities. He wants us to use them for him in the best way we can.

For younger children:
This activity should work equally well with all ages. Supervision of glue, scissors, etc. will be the main issue.

77

On the mountain

Matthew 17:1-9; Mark 9:2-9; Luke 9:28-36

Key verse: After six days Jesus took Peter, James and John
with him and led them up a high mountain
where they were all alone. There he was transfig-
ured before them (Mark 9:2).

Themes: Jesus; worship.

Aim: To introduce the topic of mountains prior to the
story of the transfiguration.

Preparation:

Prepare a list of famous mountains, some biblical, some
non-biblical and a list of terms which are not mountains at
all, but silly names or expressions For example:

Biblical	*Non-biblical*	*Silly*
Mt Carmel	Mt Everest	Mountain of homework
Mt Sinai	Mt Snowdon	Mountain of chocolate
Mt Horeb	Mt Kenya	European Butter Mountain
Mt of Olives	Mt Bruce	A large amount
Mt Zion	Mt Kilimanjaro	Mount a horse

How to play:

Designate one corner of the room 'Bible mountains',
another 'Other famous mountains' and a third 'not mountains at all'. Call out your list one at a time. Children choose
which type of mountain has been called and run to the
correct corner of the room. For bonus points, older children
may be able to tell you who is connected with each Bible
mountain and the locations of the other famous mountains.

Answers

Mt Carmel	1 Kings 18:19	(Elijah)
Mt Sinai	Exodus 19:20	(Moses)
Mt Horeb	Exodus 3:1	(Moses)
Mt of Olives	Acts 1:12	(Jesus)
Mt Zion	Hebrews 12:22	(Christians)
Mt Everest	(Nepal)	
Mt Snowdon	(Wales)	
Mt Kenya	(Kenya)	
Mt Bruce	(Australia)	
Mt Kilimanjaro	(Tanzania)	

Who has ever been to the top of a mountain? If the weather is fine you will see an amazing view. It will have been hard work walking to the top and you'll feel pleased you've made it at last.

Have you ever heard anyone talk about a 'mountain top experience'? A mountain top experience describes something amazing and wonderful. Several people in the Bible had some real 'mountain top experiences' that happened at the top of real mountains.

The passage today is about a mountain top experience of Peter, James and John.

For younger children:
Young children will not have sufficient biblical or geographical knowledge to successfully attempt the above game. Lead them through play-acting a journey up a mountain. First, all get ready by pretending to put on your boots, a coat and a rucksack. Talk about the different terrain, how it's getting steeper, how you have to jump a stream, etc. and stop for a rest and a drink. When you get to the top, look at the amazing view. What can you see?

78

Clear out!

Matthew 21:12-13; Mark 11:15-17; John 2:13-22

Key verse: Jesus entered the temple area and drove out all
who were buying and selling there. He over-
turned the tables of the moneychangers and the
benches of those selling doves (Matthew 21:12).

Themes: The temple; holiness; anger; sin; Jesus.

Aim: To teach about righteous anger.

Preparation:

You will need some plastic money or about 20 'coins' made
from silver card or similar. You will also need a stopwatch.
Mark out a rectangle with chalk or masking tape, as big as
you can make it while still allowing about one metre of space
around the edge. You may need to go outside so that you
have enough room for this game. Spread the 'coins' around
the area.

How to play:

This is an adapted version of 'tag'. One person is 'It' whilst
everyone else tries to avoid being tagged by her.

Everyone must stay inside the marked area. If they go
outside the rectangle they are 'out' and must stay there. If
they are tagged they are also 'out' and must go outside the
area. The person who is 'It' must try to get everyone 'out'. In
addition she must remove all the coins from the playing area.
Time how long it takes for the area to be cleared of people
and money. Then play a second and third round with a different person as 'It'. Choose energetic children to be 'It'.

If she has difficulty in catching all the players, add in a second 'It' or a leader to assist.

When Jesus went to the temple, he found money-changers who were cheating people and animal sellers charging too much. And all this was happening in a part of the temple that should have been used for prayer! Jesus was angry.

He drove out all the people and their animals.

For younger children:
Choose a leader to be 'It' for this game.

Children could pretend to be doves or sheep. On all fours, the sheep at least would be easier for the leader to catch!

79

Pass the Parcel Prayer

Matthew 6:9-13; Luke 11:1-4

Key verse: 'This, then, is how you should pray: Our Father in heaven, hallowed be your name …' (Matthew 6:9).

Themes: Prayer; Jesus.

Aim: To help the children remember the Lord's Prayer.

Preparation:

Wrap up a small prize in seven layers of paper. In each layer place a piece of card on which is written part of the Lord's Prayer with a few words missing, e.g. Outermost layer: 'Our Father _____ hallowed _____ '; Inner layer: 'but _____ from _____ .'

How to play:

Play this game in traditional 'Pass the Parcel' style. When the music stops, the child holding the parcel takes off one layer and tries to complete the part of the prayer written on the card they find.

If successful, they can be rewarded with a sticker or sweet. If not, they pass the card to their left until someone successfully completes the sentence. (For older children, you could ask for an explanation of the sentence as well.)

This is how Jesus taught us to pray. We don't have to use the exact words. The prayer is a pattern or model to help us. If we remember the parts of this prayer, it will

help us to remember several things when we pray, for example, that we can talk to God as our Father and that prayer is not just about giving God a 'shopping list' of things we want. It's about asking for forgiveness, protection and God's will to be done.

For younger children:
Simply write the words out in full. If a child cannot yet read the words, he/she can repeat the words after a leader.

80

Continuous Relay

Luke 11:5-13; 18:1-8; 1 Thessalonians 5:17
Key verse: Pray continually (1 Thessalonians 5:17).
Theme: Prayer.
Aim: To help the children remember that we can and should pray often throughout the day.

Preparation:
Collect together a variety of unbreakable objects that represent different times of day, for example, an alarm clock, a packet of breakfast cereal, a toothbrush, a toy car, a school book, a lunch box, a football, a pillow.

You will need similar objects for each team; at least enough for every child to run twice.

How to play:
Position the children, in teams, with their objects, at one end of the room. The game consists of a continuous relay: One child in each team runs with their first object to the other end of the room, leaves it there and runs back.

The next child does the same with the second object, and so on. When all the objects have been left at the other end of the room, children then begin to retrieve them when they run. The race finishes when one team has retrieved all their objects.

The type of relay you just completed is called a 'continuous relay' – you didn't just run once each but kept going continually.

The Bible tells us to pray continually. All these objects could represent a different time of day (talk about the times they could represent). God likes to answer our prayers but we must keep praying and not give up.

For younger children:
Young children may not understand the concept of a relay. Instead, sit the children in a circle and pass one object round. Then, add in another object, then another. See how many objects you can keep moving round the circle at the same time without dropping one.

81

Prayer Warfare

John 17:1-26 Jesus prays

Key verse: My prayer is not that you take them out of the world but that you protect them from the evil one (John 17:15).

Theme: Prayer.

Aim: To understand that it is not always easy to pray and that prayer can be like fighting a battle.

Preparation:

You will need a large quantity of sheets of newspaper. You will also need a chair in the middle of the room and two long lines drawn or taped across the floor at either end of the room.

How to play:

Divide the group into two teams, A and B:

• Team A: Stand one person on the chair in the middle of the room. Stand a few of the team behind one of the lines and a few behind the other line. Half of the team must make and throw newspaper balls to the person on the chair. This person must catch as many as possible and throw them to the rest of the team standing behind the other line. They catch them and collect them in a bucket. They must not collect newspaper balls that have not reached the area behind their line.

• Team B: Members of Team B stand in the space between the two lines. They must try to prevent newspaper balls reaching the person on the chair. They are not allowed to catch newspaper balls but must deflect them so that they land in the space between the two lines from where Team A cannot retrieve them.

Play for two minutes and then have the teams swap roles. The team collecting the most newspaper balls in their bucket is the winner.

The players throwing newspaper balls represent people praying. The person on the chair represents God. The players collecting the newspaper balls represent people being prayed for. The people deflecting the newspaper balls show that prayer includes an element of spiritual warfare.

The devil does not like people to pray so it can be hard work. When Jesus prayed for his disciples just before he died, he prayed for their protection from the evil one as he knew they would face a spiritual battle as they followed him.

For younger children:
Play a throwing and catching game to illustrate how prayer works. Use a large ball or balloons to make the catching as easy as possible. (If the children are very young, just pass the ball without throwing.)

For example, have a leader stand in a hoop to represent God. God gives us good things and we can say thank you *(Leader throws ball to player 1 who catches it and throws it back).*

We can pray for ourselves and God answers *(Player 1 throws ball to Leader who catches it and throws it back).*

We can pray for someone else *(Player 1 throws ball to Leader who catches it and throws it to Player 2).*

Someone else can pray for us *(Player 2 throws ball to Leader who catches it and throws it to Player 1).*

82

Well Connected

John 15:1-8

Key verse: I am the vine; you are the branches. If a man remains in me and I in him, he will bear much fruit; apart from me you can do nothing (John 15:5).

Themes: Jesus; promises.

Aim: To introduce the topic of connections, leading on to teaching about Jesus as the vine.

Preparation:

You will need a die and a clean handkerchief on a table.

How to play:

This game involves connections between team members. It will work best if you can form two single-sex teams of equal numbers with four or more in each group. You can adjust the game to suit your group if this is not possible.

Each team must stand side by side in a straight line holding hands facing the other team. The last person in each team must be standing near a table. On the table should be one clean handkerchief, within easy reach of the last team members.

To start the game, a leader throws a die so that the first team member in each team can see it. Everyone else must look away, towards the table. If it lands on an odd number, the first person in the girls' team must squeeze the hand of the girl next to her, who squeezes the hand of the girl next to her, and so on down the team. As soon as the last girl feels her hand squeezed, she must grab the handkerchief. If it lands on an even number, the boys' team must squeeze hands in the same way. If it lands on a one or a six, both teams should squeeze hands and race to grab the handkerchief first. Points are added when teams pick up the handkerchief correctly, with bonus points for being first when they race, and deducted for mistaken squeezing and grabbing.

Make sure that a good prize is at stake, in case your group is reluctant to hold hands.

To do well in this game, you need good connections between team members. You have to be alert and only squeeze hands at the right time. If one person does it wrong, the team will lose. Jesus spoke about us being connected to him. He said he is like the vine and we are like the branches. We will only bear fruit if we are connected to him.

For younger children:
The vine, branches and fruit illustration will be a little hard for young children to grasp. You may be able to help them understand by talking about electricity. Stand the children in a long line holding hands. Tell them that the child at one end of the line is the 'switch' and the child at the other end is the 'lamp'.

When you move the 'switch' (if they hold one hand in the air, you can pull it downwards), they must squeeze the hand of the child next to them, who squeezes the hand of the next child, and so on down the line until the 'lamp' is 'lit' (this child can hold out both arms). After a couple of practices, time the children several times and see how quickly they can pass the 'current' down the line. You can then move on to show a picture of a vine and talk about Jesus' illustration and what it means.

83

In remembrance

Luke 22:7-20; Matthew 26:17-30; Mark 14:12-26

Key verse: And he took bread, gave thanks and broke it, and gave it to them, saying, 'This is my body given for you; do this in remembrance of me' (Luke 22:19).

Themes: Jesus; Easter.

Aim: To introduce the topic of remembering, prior to talking about why we share bread and wine to remember Jesus.

Preparation:

You will need a selection of objects to do with 'remembering'. For example: Birthday cake candles; an anniversary card; a theatre programme; a photo; several souvenir items such as an Isle of Wight pencil, a science museum sticker or an Edinburgh Castle badge. Aim for about 20 items altogether.

How to play:

Place all the objects on a tray and cover them with a cloth. Uncover the tray for 30 seconds and allow everyone to have a look and try to remember what they see. Then cover it up again. Allow pairs two minutes to write a list of all they can remember.

When the time is up, check how many they all have and then give a quick clue for each object so that they have a chance to complete their list.

Give clues such as pretending to blow out candles or to open an envelope.

Reminders are useful if we want to remember things. I gave you a reminder for each object to help you to remember it. Each of the objects themselves are reminders too. This theatre programme reminds me of the show I went to see last year. This photo reminds me of our trip to London. This pencil reminds me of my holiday to the Isle of Wight.

Jesus wanted the disciples to remember him and his death and resurrection. At the Last Supper he shared out bread and wine and told them to remember him. Now 2000 years on we still share bread and wine to remember Jesus.

For younger children:
This activity is suitable for all ages, although you may wish to reduce the number of items for younger children.

84

Perfect!

John 18:28-40; 19:1-16; Matthew 27:11-26; Mark 15:1-15;
Luke 23:1-23

Key verse: Once more Pilate came out and said to the Jews,
'Look, I am bringing him out to you to let you
know that I find no basis for a charge against
him' (John 19:4).

Themes: Jesus; Easter; sin.

Aim: To help the children to understand the concept
of perfection. We do not live perfect lives, but
Jesus did.

Preparation:
Position several tables around the room. On each table set up
a different activity linked with the theme of perfection.
Example activities:
• Provide paper and pencils. Draw a perfect circle.
• Provide plasticine or play dough. Make a perfect cube.
• Provide pictures of people with different hairstyles. Who
  has 'perfect' hair?
• Provide pictures of people smiling. Who has 'perfect'
  teeth?
• Provide a selection of white objects. Which is a perfect,
  pure white?

How to play:
Ask everyone to work their way around the tables, having a
go at each activity. Afterwards, see whether anyone managed
to draw a perfect circle or make a perfect cube (unlikely) and

discuss who people think has perfect hair or teeth and which object is perfectly white. What does 'perfect' mean? (E.g. ideal, faultless, flawless, spotless, impeccable, immaculate, nothing wrong, just right.) Can perfection be a matter of opinion?

Certain shapes can be perfect. A certain aspect of someone may be thought of as perfect by some people. In God's eyes, no one is perfect. Everybody does things wrong. Everybody sins.

Jesus, God's son, is the only perfect person who has ever lived. Pilate said he could find 'no basis for a charge against him'. He did not realise the full truth of what he said!

Our sins are a problem because God cannot accept people who are not perfect and holy like he is. If there was no answer to that problem it would mean no one could get to know God and no one could go to be with him when they die. Jesus can make us perfect in God's eyes.

For younger children:
If you have a leader to explain each of the five activities, you could do these with younger children too. If not, see who can draw the 'nearest to perfect' circle, square, triangle and straight line.

85

Pass the guard

Luke 24:1-12; Matthew 27:62-66; 28:1-15; Mark 16:1-14; John 20:1-9

Key verse: When the chief priests had met with the elders and devised a plan, they gave the soldiers a large sum of money, telling them, 'You are to say, "His disciples came during the night and stole him away while we were asleep"'(Matthew 28:12-13).

Themes: Jesus; Easter; Miracles.

Aim: To help the children understand that the only explanation for the empty tomb is that Jesus rose from the dead.

Preparation:
Make a simple obstacle course across your playing space.

How to play:
Choose a volunteer to stand facing the far wall, as a guard. Others stand at the start of the course.

Silently signal children to commence the course. They must try and reach the guard, who can turn round at any moment. When seen, moving children must sit down. Change the guard to re-commence the game.

Some people think that Jesus never really died in the first place. Do you think it's possible that Jesus, tightly wrapped up in bandages and extremely badly hurt could push the huge stone from the tomb's entrance, and sneak past first-class Roman soldiers? Do you think

the disciples could have sneaked past the guards to rescue him? No. Jesus was dead, but God's great power brought him back to life again.

For younger children:
Adjust the difficulty of the obstacles, or remove them altogether, depending on the age of the children.

86

Eggs, eggs, eggs!

Luke 24:1-12; Matthew 27:62-66; 28:1-15; Mark 16:1-14; John 20:1-9

Key verse: He is not here; he has risen! Remember how he told you, while he was still with you in Galilee: 'The Son of Man must be delivered into the hands of sinful men, be crucified and on the third day be raised again' (Luke 24:6-7).

Themes: Jesus; Easter.

Aim: To help children see the link between our traditional, and often rather secular, way of celebrating Easter with the new life we have through the death and resurrection of Jesus.

Preparation:

You will need spoons and hard-boiled eggs, fresh eggs and a large quantity of chocolate mini-eggs. Hide the mini-eggs around your room, building and/or grounds.

How to play:

1. Hold traditional egg and spoon races.
2. Older children can try egg catching – they will need to go outside. How far apart can they get whilst still able to catch a fresh egg? (You may like to give them aprons for this!)
3. Organise an egg hunt using the mini-eggs.

Very early in Christian tradition, eggs became associated with Easter. People thought they looked like the tomb

in which Jesus was placed. New life emerges from an egg, and Jesus came out of the tomb alive.

For younger children:
Omit game 2.

87

Hand ID

John 20:24-29

Key verse: But he said to them, 'Unless I see the nail marks
                 in his hands and put my finger where the nails
                 were, and put my hand into his side, I will not
                 believe it' (John 20:25).

Themes: Jesus; faith; Easter.

Aim: To help the children remember the story of
                 Thomas and his desire for proof of Jesus' resur-
                 rection.

Preparation:

You will need a few adults and/or older children, including if
possible parents and/or siblings of several children, and a
low screen for them to kneel behind where the children can't
see them.

How to play:

Ask the children to look carefully at their hands and those of
a friend – the backs, the fronts, the fingernails and lines.
Everyone's hands are different. Then send volunteers round
behind the screen, and ask them to hold one hand up so that
the children can see it. The children can walk past in front of
the screen looking at the hands to see whether they can
recognise any of them.

Alternatively, you could ask children's partners to go
behind the screen for children to try to identify.

Everyone's hands are different. Jesus' disciples saw him use his hands every day. They watched his hands help and heal people. They saw his hands nailed to the cross. When he was alive again, Jesus told them to look at his hands, and touch them. They saw the nail prints, too, and knew it was Jesus. He was alive!

For younger children:
Have an adult draw round the children's hands on separate pieces of paper, all in the same colour. Mix up the papers and let children try to find their own hand pictures by placing their hands in the outlines.

88

Gone fishing

John 21:1-19; Luke 5:1-11

Key verse: He said, 'Throw your net on the right side of the
              boat and you will find some.' When they did,
              they were unable to haul the net in because of
              the large number of fish (John 21:6).

Themes: Miracles; mission; Jesus; Easter.

Aim: To help the children remember the story of the
              miraculous catch of fish after Jesus' resurrec-
              tion, and of Jesus' promise to his disciples when
              he first called them, that they would become
              'fishers of men' — i.e. evangelize with success.

Preparation:

You will need a large container to act as a 'fish tank' and a
large number of cardboard fish each with a paper clip
attached to its mouth. Fish should have a number written on
the face down side – 5, 10 or 20.

You will also need a few 'fishing rods' made from sticks
and a piece of string with a small magnet on the end.

How to play:

Form teams and ask questions such as the following:

- Give a type of fish named after something in the story of
  Noah. *(Rainbow trout.)*
- How many fish did Jesus use, with some loaves, to feed
  five thousand people? *(Two.)*
- Who was swallowed by a big fish somewhere between
  Joppa and Tarshish? *(Jonah.)*

- Give a type of fish named after something in the story of Jesus' birth. *(Star fish.)*
- What do we call a large group of fish? *(Shoal or school.)*
- How do fish breathe? *(With gills.)*
- Give a type of fish whose name is the same as an item of party food. *(Jelly fish.)*
- Name a type of fish with spines on its back that you might catch in a stream. *(Stickleback.)*
- Name a type of fish that you might expect to ride on. *(Sea horse.)*
- Which type of fish climbs ladders? *(Salmon.)*
- What sort of shellfish would you find in a cocktail? *(Prawn.)*
- What type of fish is a whale? *(It's not a fish, it's a mammal.)*

The first team to answer correctly chooses one team member to run to the front where there will be a large 'fish tank' containing cardboard fish. The team member takes a rod and pulls out a fish. The number on the fish corresponds to the number of points won. The fish is taken back to the team.

At the end of the quiz, the points on the fish are counted. The winning team will not necessarily be the one with the most correct questions, as point totals will also depend on their luck at the fish tank.

After his resurrection Jesus appeared to his disciples while they were on an unsuccessful fishing trip. Jesus told them to try again on the other side of the boat and they caught a miraculous number of fish.

Three years before, Simon Peter had been on an unsuccessful fishing trip when Jesus met him and told him to try again. That time also he had caught a miraculous number of fish.

On that occasion Jesus first told Peter to follow him and that he would now be an evangelist, calling people to follow Jesus. This time, after Peter's denials, Jesus called him again to follow him. He calls us to follow him too and witness for him.

For younger children:
Make up simpler questions or just use the fishing part as a game.

89

Believer, doubter, unbeliever

Matthew 27 & 28; Mark 15 & 16; Luke 23 & 24; John 18-21.

Key verse: Then Jesus told him, 'Because you have seen me, you have believed; blessed are those who have not seen and yet have believed' (John 20:29).

Themes: Faith; Jesus; Easter.

Aim: To think about how people react to Jesus through the story of Easter week featuring those who did not believe Jesus, those who did believe and those who doubted.

Preparation:

You will need a bench, low wall, or plank raised slightly from the floor. A straight line would do if you can't manage one of these. Write yourself a list of names to use in the game:

• Believers – Mary, Jesus' mother; Peter; John; Joseph of Arimathea; Nicodemus; Mary Magdalene; Salome, Joanna.

• Unbelievers – Annas; Caiaphas; Pilate; Jewish leaders; soldiers.

• Doubter: Thomas.

How to play:

Allow about four children to play at a time. You can have heats and a final. The four children stand on the bench. Have an adult holding each end of the bench in case of any unstability as they jump on and off. Designate one side of the bench 'believers' and the other side 'unbelievers'. Call out one of your names. If he/she is a believer the children jump onto the floor on the 'believers' side. If an unbeliever they jump off onto the 'unbelievers' side. If you call 'Thomas' they must stand still on the bench. If children jump onto the wrong side or fall off when you call 'Thomas' they are 'out'.

You may need to speed up the game to find a winner. Heat winners can compete in the final at the end.

The leaders and people in power in Jesus' time did not believe Jesus was God's Son. They did not believe his miracles were from God. They thought he was a troublemaker and wanted to get rid of him. They made up lies and turned people against him in order to have him crucified.

Jesus' disciples, his mother and several other women were devoted followers of Jesus. Although at the time of his arrest we see them run away in fear, we see several of them at the cross and tomb. After his resurrection, the women were the first to believe he had risen.

The last of the disciples to believe was Thomas who had not been with the other disciples when they saw Jesus alive and insisted on seeing for himself.

For younger children:
Use just a few simple names: Mary, Peter, John, Pilate, high priest, Jews, Thomas.

Use a line instead of a bench and have all the children jumping together.

90

Disciple-making relay

Matthew 28:16-20; Mark 16:15-20; Luke 24:44-49

Key verse: Therefore go and make disciples of all nations,
baptising them in the name of the Father and of
the Son and of the Holy Spirit, and teaching
them to obey everything I have commanded you
(Matthew 28:19-20).

Themes: Discipleship; mission; Jesus.

Aim: To help the children understand some of what is
involved in becoming and making disciples of
Jesus.

Preparation:

You will need a Bible, a map, a cardboard heart and a battery
for each team. Place them at the opposite end of the room
to your start line.

How to play:

Children form teams of four and run in turn relay-style to
collect their objects one by one. Add obstacles to make the
race more interesting.

**Jesus told his disciples to make more disciples. To be
disciples we need God's word, the Bible, so that we
know what Jesus wants to teach us.**

**We need God's love (heart) so that we can love oth-
ers. We need power from God (battery), his Holy Spirit
living in us.**

And if we're going to make more disciples from all

nations, as Jesus has asked us to, we'll also need a map to help us find the way!

In Bible times, Jesus' disciples travelled many miles to many countries telling people about him and making disciples.

For younger children:
Simply hide objects round the room for children to find if you think they won't understand the concept of a relay.

91

Pentecost Power

Acts 1:1-8; 2:1-41

Key verse: In the last days, God says, I will pour out my
Spirit on all people (Acts 2:17).

Themes: Holy Spirit; miracles.

Aim: To help the children understand more about the
Holy Spirit.

Preparation: You will need drinking straws; ping-pong balls;
several torches (taken apart) or sets of batteries, wires and
small bulbs.

How to play:

Form teams of three or four. The activity consists of two
parts:

- Teams race to assemble a torch or simple circuit
- When a team's torch or bulb is lit, this is the signal for one
  team member to start to blow through a drinking straw to
  propel a table tennis ball between two lines marked on the
  floor. First to the end wins.

**The sort of power that made the bulb light is electric
power. You can't see the actual electricity going through
the wires but you can see its effect and we know the
power comes from the battery. Your lung power made
the ping-pong ball move. You can't see your breath as it
goes through the straw but you can see its effect. We
know the power comes from your lungs.**

After Jesus went back to be with his Father, he sent

the Holy Spirit. The Holy Spirit enabled the power of God to work through the disciples.

We can't see the power of the Holy Spirit but we can see its effect – for example, the disciples saw people healed and raised from the dead; they saw demons driven out; they saw thousands repent and become Christians; they were able to speak in languages they had never learned.

All other people who have begun to follow Jesus since that time can experience the power of God through the Holy Spirit.

For younger children:
Omit the competitive element and have leaders help small groups of children to assemble the torches and blow through the straws.

92

To the ends of the earth

Acts 1:1-8; 2:1-41

Key verse: But you will receive power when the Holy Spirit comes on you; and you will be my witnesses in Jerusalem, and in all Judea and Samaria, and to the ends of the earth (Acts 1:8).

Themes: Holy Spirit; mission; Jesus.

Aim: To help the children remember Jesus' command to be his witnesses all over the world.

Preparation:

Mark a large circle away from the walls, but towards one end, of your playing area. All of your group should be able to stand in the middle of it with plenty of room to spare. You will need a stopwatch.

How to play:

Form two teams. One team watches while the other plays. They then swap over.

Explain that the middle of your circle represents Jerusalem; the edge of your circle represents Judea; the wall or line nearest to the circle represents Samaria; the wall or line furthest from your circle represents 'the ends of the earth'.

Team A starts in Jerusalem. Start a stopwatch and call out the locations randomly. The team runs to each place. When everyone is there, call the next place. After several turns, call out instructions such as 'two to Samaria, five to Judea', then 'four to Jerusalem, three to the ends of the earth' (these numbers are appropriate to seven in a team, so everyone goes somewhere). End with 'all to Jerusalem'. Stop the stopwatch and note the time.

Team B then plays in a similar fashion. Make sure you give the same number of very similar instructions (but not identical), so that the game is fair.

Jesus wanted his disciples to tell people everywhere about him. They were to start in Jerusalem and then go throughout the region of Judea and neighbouring Samaria and all over the world. The disciples, plus other people who became Jesus' followers, travelled all over the world. Even now, two thousand years later, we can all be disciples and part of the same process, telling people about Jesus.

For younger children:
All the team should run to the same place each time to avoid confusion.

93

Stick together!

Acts 2:42-47

Key verse: And the Lord added to their number daily those who were being saved (Acts 2:47).

Themes: Sharing; church.

Aim: To help the children remember how the early church grew and stuck together.

How to play:

Form equal teams of six or more. Half the team should stand at one end of the playing area and the other half at the other end. On the word 'Go!' one team member from each team runs to meet the rest of their team. They grasp the hand of one of their teammates and together they run back to the other half of the team. Here they grasp hands with another teammate and all three run back together to the other end.

This continues until the whole team is holding hands and has completed a length of the course. Make sure the course isn't too long otherwise the first couple of people will be exhausted!

In that relay you had to keep adding people to your team and all stick together.

In the book of Acts we read that every day more and more people were being added to the early church in Jerusalem. They stuck together, making good friendships, learning from Jesus' disciples, praying, breaking bread together, praising God and sharing their money

and possessions. **All over the world the church is still growing and God wants us to stick together and support each other in our daily lives and our work for him.**

For younger children:
An alternative would be to gradually make a long conga line, dancing and singing along to some children's praise music.

94

World of Food

Acts 10:1-48

Key verse: Then Peter began to speak: 'I now realise how true it is that God does not show favouritism but accepts men from every nation who fear him and do what is right ' (Acts 10:34-35).

Theme: Mission.

Aim: To help the children remember God's message to Peter about accepting people from every nation.

Preparation:

You will need to collect a variety of foods from different countries. Large supermarkets stock plenty.

Examples: Pizza from Italy; bread from France; prawn crackers from China; yoghurt from Greece; coconut from Hawaii.

How to play:

Check for food allergies before you start. Lay out small samples of each food. Ask volunteers to taste each food and guess where it comes from. If you think that they will find this difficult, give them a choice of three countries.

To make it more difficult, blindfold the volunteers so that they have to identify the food as well as the country. Award points for correct answers and give a prize to the winner, e.g. make and present a voucher for a free fish and chips meal. Have a world map handy and award extra points if children can find the countries they name on the map.

For Peter, the type of food he could and couldn't eat was an essential part of being a Jew. Jews didn't even eat at the same table as non-Jews, let alone eat the same foods.

However, God told him that these food rules were not important for Christians – people who ate any sort of food were acceptable to him. Peter was learning about what was essential for a Christian and what was not. He did not need to force people like Cornelius into obeying Jewish laws.

Similarly, people who become Christians nowadays don't have to eat the same food as us, dress like us, or sing the same songs as us. The Bible makes it clear that the essential thing is to repent and accept Jesus as Saviour and Lord of our lives.

For younger children:

Young children may be less adventurous with the types of food they are willing to try. You may wish to avoid the food option altogether and play a game about differences.

Stand in a circle with a leader in the middle.

Call out a category such as 'Wearing blue'. (All those wearing blue collect a small piece of card or a small sticker).

Call out another category such as 'name begins with B'. All those with a name beginning with B can go to the leader in the middle and collect a point.

Continue for as long as appropriate, ensuring everyone gets at least a couple of points. You could give a small prize to the 'winning' child, although you will point out that it was just luck – there was nothing better about that person compared with the rest of them.

95

Unchained

Acts 12:1-17

Key verse: Suddenly an angel of the Lord appeared and a light shone in the cell. He struck Peter on the side and woke him up. 'Quick, get up!' he said, and the chains fell off Peter's wrists (Acts 12:7).

Themes: Church; prayer; miracles.

Aim: To help the children remember the story of Peter's miraculous escape from prison.

Preparation:
You will need about one metre of string per child. You will also need to practice!

How to play:
Form pairs of children. Loosely tie a piece of string around one child's wrists, a loop on each wrist, leaving plenty of string between their wrists. It should look a little like hand-cuffs. Do the same with the second child of each pair, but before tying the second wrist, take the string behind the string of the first child, so that they end up linked together.

The challenge is for pairs to separate without cutting the string.

The answer is to thread a length of the between-wrist string up through one of the other person's wrist loops from the elbow side, and then over that hand. Show the children how to do this – most won't manage on their own. They'll have fun later showing their parents.

Peter was put in prison for talking to people about Jesus. He was chained in a cell with two soldiers to guard him. One night an angel appeared and his chains fell off. There was no special trick that the angel used, like the one we just used to escape from the string hand-cuffs. It was supernatural power from God that made the chains fall off and the prison doors open and enabled Peter to walk out to freedom without being seen.

For younger children:
Tie a couple of leaders as above and let the children suggest ways for them to get free. Ideally have two pairs of leaders and two groups of children so they can race.

96

All change

Acts 9:1-19

Key verse: Placing his hands on Saul he said, 'Brother Saul, the Lord – Jesus, who appeared to you on the road as you were coming here – has sent me so that you may see again and be filled with the Holy Spirit' (Acts 9:17).

Theme: Salvation.

Aim: To reinforce the fact that when someone becomes a Christian they undergo a radical change on the inside, as happened to Saul.

Preparation:

Collect pairs of photographs (or photocopies of photographs) of people well known to the children. One of each pair of photographs must feature the person several, or many, years ago. The other must be recent. You could use pictures of celebrities as well as those of church members and of children's families. Label each with a letter and stick them up around the room. Pairs of children will need pencil and paper between them.

How to play:

In pairs, children go round the room with pencil and paper matching up as many pairs of photographs as possible.

Everyone changes. On the outside, people sometimes change so much that you can't recognise them. Some of those photographs were hard to match up! But the

outside isn't very important. The inside matters most. People change on the inside too. Saul, or Paul as he was later known, changed on the inside. To start with, he hated Christians and wanted to kill them. Then he met Jesus and realised how wrong he had been. He received the Holy Spirit and became one of the first people to start churches.

Everyone changes on the inside when they become a Christian. We say no to sin and begin to follow Jesus, like Paul did.

For younger children:
Leaders will need to go round with small groups of children. Remember young children aren't very tall so don't put the photographs too high. Use fewer photographs. Photographs of the children themselves will be easier to guess.

97

Paul's adventures

Acts 9, 13 – 15

Key verse: While they were worshipping the Lord and fast-
ing, the Holy Spirit said, 'Set apart Barnabas and
Saul for the work to which I have called them'
(Acts 13:2).

Themes: Mission; miracles.

Aim: To help the children remember some of Paul's
adventures as he travelled preaching the gospel.

Preparation:

You will need to set up various stations around your room,
each representing part of Paul's travels.

Start – Provide a die.

Station 1 – Provide a box or tunnel that children climb
through.

Station 2 – Provide a blindfold.

Station 3 – Provide a chair and Acts 13:14 written out.

Station 4 – Provide a bucket and some stones.

Station 5 – Provide Acts 15:4 written out.

Station 6 – Mark a finish line.

Each station will need an instruction card, explaining
what to do (see below). You will also need a stopwatch.

How to play:

Demonstrate how the course should be followed. Time children to complete the course. Once one child has passed a
couple of stations you could start the next one with another
leader supervising and timing him/her.

Start   Paul's conversion.

Throw a six to begin and move to Station 1.

Station 1 Damascus.

Jews try to kill Paul. Paul escapes through the wall in a basket. Crawl through the tunnel.

Station 2 Cyprus.

Paul meets a sorcerer who opposes him but God blinds the man. Have your leader lead you blind-folded to Station 3.

Station 3 Pisidian Antioch

Paul sits and preaches in the synagogue. Read out Acts 13:14 before moving on.

Station 4 Iconium, Lystra and Derbe

A lame man is healed. Do five squat jumps. Paul faces opposition and is stoned. Throw five stones into the bucket.

Station 5 Jerusalem

Paul reports back to Jerusalem and talks with Peter and the other leaders there. Read out Acts 15:4 before moving on.

Station 6 Antioch.

Paul stayed here teaching the new church.

Paul went to many places to tell them about Jesus. Often a church was started as a result of his preaching and teaching. The journeys were difficult and he often faced opposition but Jesus helped Paul to accomplish all that he had given him to do.

For younger children:
A leader can accompany a small group of children through the course, explain each station carefully, and read the verses for them. Omit the timing.

98

Prisoners

Acts 16:16-40

Key verse: Suddenly there was such a violent earthquake that the foundations of the prison were shaken. At once all the prison doors flew open, and everybody's chains came loose (Acts 16:26).

Theme: Miracles.

Aim: To help the children remember the story of Paul and Silas in prison.

Preparation:

You will need several soft balls.

How to play:

Form two teams. One team will represent 'jailers' and the other will be 'prisoners'. Jailers stand down the two long sides of the rectangular playing area, opposite each other, holding the balls. Prisoners stand at one of the shorter ends of the playing area.

On the word 'Go!' prisoners run to the other end of the area. Meanwhile jailers throw the balls at the prisoners' feet and lower legs. Any prisoners touched with a ball are 'in jail' and must sit down at one end. This is repeated for several minutes so that most of the prisoners are in jail.

After a set time, e.g. three minutes, call 'earthquake'. At this point jailers and prisoners swap roles. See whether the new jailers can put their prisoners in jail any faster than the first group of jailers.

Paul and Silas were put in prison after they cast an evil spirit out of a slave girl in Philippi. However, as they were praising God in prison, an earthquake caused their chains to come loose and the doors to fly open.

The jailer was terrified as he thought the prisoners would escape and he would be executed. But Paul and Silas didn't run away. They stayed to explain about Jesus to the jailer and his family.

The jailer and his family became Christians. In the morning the magistrates ordered that Paul and Silas be released.

For younger children:
Sit the children on chairs arranged in a circle, with gaps left between them. Call out instructions such as 'Praise God' (sing a verse of a song together); 'In prison' (sit on the chairs); 'Chains loose' (jump up); 'Earthquake' (run round outside the circle of chairs).

99

Shipwreck

Acts 27:1-44

Key verse: Last night an angel of the God whose I am and whom I serve stood beside me and said, 'Do not be afraid, Paul. You must stand trial before Caesar; and God has graciously given you the lives of all who sail with you (Acts 27:23-24).

Theme: Mission.

Aim: To help the children remember the story of Paul's shipwreck.

Preparation:
Prepare a list of instructions to help you (see below).

How to play:
This is an adapted version of 'Captain's Calling'. The four sides of your playing area represent port (to the left), starboard (to the right), fore (to the front) and aft (to the rear). On these commands, children run to the appropriate side. The last few children to the sides each time are 'out'.

Other commands, for which children perform actions, include 'climb the rigging' (pretend to climb); 'man the lifeboats' (get into pairs and row); sharks! (jump into a partner's arms); man overboard! (swim quickly); Captain's coming (stand and salute).

To finish the game shout 'Shipwreck!' First child to reach 'shore' (any wall) wins.

Paul had been arrested in Jerusalem and the Romans decided he should be sent to Caesar in Rome to have his case heard. This involved a long, dangerous journey by ship. The voyage was eventful and they were shipwrecked, but God did not let anyone drown. Even as a prisoner Paul told the soldiers, sailors and islanders about Jesus.

For younger children:
It will be helpful if one or two leaders join in to assist the children in remembering a reduced selection of actions and which wall is which.

100

Letter race

Romans 1:1-7; 1 Corinthians 1:1-3; Galatians 1:1-5;
Ephesians 1:1-2; Philippians 1:1-2

Key verse: To the church of God in Corinth, to those sanc-
tified in Christ Jesus and called to be holy,
together with all those everywhere who call on
the name of our Lord Jesus Christ – their Lord
and ours (1 Corinthians 1:2).

Themes: Mission; church.

Aim: To help the children remember how Paul wrote
letters to teach and encourage people in many
places.

Preparation:

You will need

• six boxes labelled Rome, Corinth, Galatia, Ephesus,
Philippi and Colosse.

• three large name labels for three people to hold saying
Timothy, Titus and Philemon.

• nine 'scrolls' for each team labelled 'To the Romans', 'To
the Corinthians', 'To the Galatians', 'To the Philippians',
'To the Colossians', 'To Timothy', 'To Titus', 'To
Philemon'.

How to play:

Form several small teams and give each team their nine
'scrolls'. Explain that Paul has written letters to all these
places and people and that the teams must deliver them.

Show them the boxes, placed around the room, and

explain which scroll goes to which box. Give three helpers or older children the name labels and tell the teams who is who. These people will walk backwards and forwards across the room at one end.

On the word 'Go!' teams race relay-style to deliver all their scrolls.

Paul travelled to many places. He wanted to keep in touch with the new Christians in each place. They needed help to learn about Jesus and instructions about how to live their lives as Jesus' followers.

They couldn't learn everything while Paul was with them so when Paul travelled to other places he would write back to other towns and people he had visited. He also wrote letters when he was put in prison and couldn't visit anyone. We have many of these letters in the Bible.

We can read what Paul wrote two thousand years ago and learn from him, just like the people in Rome, Corinth, Galatia, Ephesus, Philippi and Colosse.

For younger children:
This game is an adaptation of 'I wrote a letter to my love'. All the children sit on the floor facing inwards. Give one child an envelope and say, 'It's for the Romans'. The child walks around the outside of the circle as a leader says, 'Paul wrote a letter to the Romans and asked a friend to take it. Is that you or you or you … it's you!'

At this point the child drops the envelope into the lap of the child beside him who gets up. Both run round the outside of the circle back to the empty place. The deliverer sits down and the second child becomes the new deliverer.

Index by theme

Holy Spirit

91 The promise of power
92 The Holy Spirit comes
   in power

Jesus

51 Jesus' birth prophesied
52 God promises
   Zechariah a son
53 An angel visits Mary
54 Joseph hears from God
57 Jesus grows up
58 Jesus is baptised
60 Jesus calls the first disciples
61 Jesus calls John, Andrew
   & Simon
64 Water into wine
65 Healing the paralysed man
66 Healing the blind man
67 Lazarus raised from the dead
68 Peter walks on water
69 Feeding 5000 people
70 Jesus & Nicodemus
71 Jesus & Zacchaeus
72 Lost sheep
73 Prodigal son
74 The sower & the seed
75 Good Samaritan
76 Parable of the talents
77 The transfiguration
78 Jesus clears the temple
79 The Lord's Prayer
82 The vine & the branches
83 The last supper
84 Jesus on trial
85 The empty tomb
86 Christ is risen
87 Thomas meets the risen Jesus
89 Responses to Easter
90 The Great Commission
92 The Holy Spirit comes
   in power

Love

37 Elijah on Mount Carmel
63 The greatest commandment
70 Jesus & Nicodemus
72 Lost sheep
73 Prodigal son
75 Good samaritan

Miracles

10 Abraham, Sarah & Isaac
18 Moses & the plagues
26 Samson
30 David & Goliath
46 Daniel's Diet
53 An angel visits Mary
64 Water into wine
65 Healing the paralysed man
66 Healing the blind man
67 Lazarus raised from the dead
68 Peter walks on water
69 Feeding 5000 people
84 Christ is risen
88 Miraculous catch of fish
91 The promise of God's power
95 Peter's escape from prison
97 Paul's missionary journeys
98 Paul & Silas in prison

Mission

56 Baby Jesus presented at the
   temple
90 The Great Commission
92 The Holy Spirit comes in
   power
94 Peter & Cornelius
97 Paul's missionary journeys
99 Paul's journey to Rome
100 Paul's letters

Obedience

6 Noah
9 Abraham
19 The Passover
20 The Ten Commandments

222

Index by Scripture

Please note the games related to gospel stories have followed various appropriate themes, rather then a strict bible passage order